David Neagle has gifted t         [barcode: T0117502]
to escape the lack conscio                    ....manity
stuck and broke for too many decades. His teachings on
manifesting our desires and creating abundant change is
both healing and empowering. David's power and ability to
breakdown the truth on how to create wealth is delivered in
a way that anyone who wants to live their full purpose, free
from financial worry, now can.

—Gina DeVee, Lifestyle Expert & Success Coach
www.EsterExperience.com

David's teachings are the gateway to prosperity. You can
struggle for years with money, but when you open this
book, open your mind to the lessons, and open your heart to
taking action you cut off any ability to be anything but your
best most abundant self. If this were mandatory reading in
high school we would all be living in a different world.

—Suzanne Evans, Author of *It's Decision Time*
www.SuzanneEvans.org

I've listened to David Neagle's *Art of Success* mp3s 11 or 12
times. That program – which is the pre-cursor to this book –
changed my life, but *The Millions Within* is 100 times better.
There is a before and an after to reading it. The before is:
broke, not sure exactly of where I wanted to take my life and
my art. The after is: making a lot of money and taking my
life and art to the level that I dreamed when I was a kid. Do
the homework. Put it into practice. It will work for you too.
And prepare to be astonished: everything happens so fast, it
is literally amazing.

—Alejandra Leibovich, Pop Surrealist Artist
www.aleloop.com

David really does have the means to bring a whole new state of creative, abundant consciousness into many people's lives so that abundance can spread further into the world until it becomes a living reality for everyone. David has been instrumental in assisting us to shift our long-held views about how to conduct our business into something that more accurately aligns us with our abilities.

—Chetan Parkyn, Author of *Human Design: Discover The Person You Were Born To Be* www.HumanDesignForUsAll.com

I love this book. There, I said it. I have personally studied with David Neagle and I have implemented many of the lessons David has decided to share with the rest of the world, in this small book. The results in my personal and professional growth have been nothing short of astounding. And I'm a lawyer. And I work with other lawyers. So we don't have much patience for "fluff." I cannot imagine a business or a profession whose owner(s) or practitioners and your clients, patients or customers would not benefit immensely from your taking very seriously the gifts of understanding and clarity David shares in this book. What David explains about "The Law of Polarity" in Chapter 7 alone warrants a serious study of this book, in my opinion.

—RJon Robins, Attorney at Law Founder, www.HowToManageASmallLawFirm.com

David Neagle has not only mastered a profound understanding of the Universal Laws, he's mastered the art of teaching them. He's got a staggering ability to take a concept that's baffled me forever and explain it in a way that suddenly (and finally!) makes the lights go on. In "The Millions Within," he pulls this magic trick over and over, giving his readers liberating clarity around what's holding them back, why they let it happen and how to blast past their conditioning to create the lives of their dreams. David is awesome. This book rocks. His readers will be extremely impressed with themselves and what they're capable of creating if they take the time to read it, absorb it and do what it says.

—Jen Sincero, Coach, Speaker and Bestselling Author of *You Are a Badass, Now Start Acting Like One: How to Stop Doubting Your Greatness and Live Large and In Charge.*
www.JenSincero.com

Are you ready to change your mental money game
from one of lack to one of abundance?
Visit **www.DavidNeagle.com** for tons of
free resources designed to teach you
how to manifest exactly what you want…
make more money ... & have an epic life!

*How To Manifest Exactly What You Want ...*
*and Have an <u>EPIC</u> Life!*

# THE MILLIONS
## Within

## DAVID NEAGLE

NEW YORK

# The Millions Within

How to Manifest Exactly What You Want…and Have an EPIC Life!

ISBN 978-1-61448-277-2 paperback
ISBN 978-1-61448-278-9-eBook
Library of Congress Control Number: 2012935710

Morgan James Publishing
The Entrepreneurial Publisher
5 Penn Plaza, 23rd Floor,
New York City, New York 10001
(212) 655-5470 office • (516) 908-4496 fax
www.MorganJamesPublishing.com

**Cover and Interior design by**
Alexander Roberts

**Back cover photo by**
Lesley Bohm

**STICKY graphics & characters designed by** Zeb

In an effort to support local communities, raise awareness and funds, Morgan James Publishing donates a percentage of all book sales for the life of each book to Habitat for Humanity Peninsula and Greater Williamsburg.

Get involved today, visit
www.MorganJamesBuilds.com.

# Contents

# ACKNOWLEDGMENTS

*To all the teachers in my life past and present,
thank you.*

*This book is dedicated to my children Ashley, Joey,
Erin and Rhiannon.*
*Thank you for choosing me to be your Dad!!*
*We have been through so much together and you
have and continue to teach me everyday how to be a
better father, a better man, and a better person.*
*It is my hope and desire that you each live the life
of your dreams and always remember that I love
each of you unconditionally and fully support
you in all you do.*

*Love Dad*

# FOREWORD

This book is not about the "airy-faerie" world of "I wish." This book is a practical guide to understanding and applying the laws of the universe to the life you want.

Famed author Arthur C. Clarke (*2001-A Space Odyssey*) postulated his now-famous "Third Law" which states: "Any sufficiently advanced technology is indistinguishable from magic." The principle being, "If you cannot explain to yourself the technology behind a thing that is OBVIOUSLY taking place the only explanation available to you is… Magic." And so it is with the masters of natural laws. These individuals appear to perform pure magic by manifesting in seemingly effortless ways things that others among us have not yet dared to imagine. It is not by *defiance* of these laws, but rather by *understanding* the laws and *applying these rules creatively* that we expand our ability to function in an orderly universe that is here, principally, to manifest the ideas of our intelligent creation.

There are many among us who have come to understand the natural and universal laws governing the production of outcomes. All of us abide by those rules because we all produce the outcomes of our lives. But the masters produce *consciously desired* outcomes… and not by fudging the laws or capitalizing on loopholes. In fact, universal laws are loophole free… like the law of gravity.

As America and other world economies undergo radical shifts the search for a magic bullet produces charlatans, snake-oil salesmen, and con men – each with their own promise of results without effort. As the Law of Polarity impresses its immutable truth upon you, so will the clear understanding that as far as results without effort goes – "there ain't no sech animal." Every re-action is produced by an action. Action MUST be taken to produce a result.

David Neagle is a student of truth, wisdom, and the law – the technology of results production. From his extensive research across an eclectic and timeless collection of astute observers and writers he has distilled the common threads of their messages and observations. In **The Millions Within,** he takes you through those very understandable rules and how you can master them in a course that could easily be called "Success 101."

This book is about succeeding… having the outcomes in your life match the desires and intentions of your mind. At the same time it must be a basic course in how the universe works, behaves, responds, and interfaces with each and all of its intelligences. As you will learn from these pages, everything you need is right around you at all times – or you wouldn't be aware you needed it in the first place! The understanding you require to operate that system is, literally, in your hands at this moment. And… like all distilled wisdom… the teachers in these pages will reveal all of the secrets, holding nothing back.

Until you are ready for these truths, however, you may look right at them, perhaps recognize them, and even clumsily utilize them – and still find yourself confounded by limited and contradictory results. This will not make the messages un-true. It will reveal the un-truths that you hold, believe in, and manifest your reality from more strongly. In this moment you are applying these rules in ways you may not see. Until you accept that it is you who are producing the result, you have no hope of altering the outcome consciously.

As you increase in harmony with these ideas, the principals will take on deeper and more far reaching meaning. Every time you come to these words with fresh eyes, you will find more here for you. The words will not change. Your understanding of them will.

What you are about to read is true. If you find yourself not liking it you must ask yourself David's hallmark question, "Why am I choosing to have this experience?" How truthfully you answer that question will, quite literally, dictate the course of your life. The good news is… you get to ask that question anytime your results don't seem to match up with your expectations. You have millions of opportunities to make a more useful course correction.

David will start you on this journey by taking you on his own discovery journey: from the very limited, frustrated character he thought he had to remain, to the unlimited person he is and continues to emerge into being. It all starts with Understanding Who You Are – and What You Want… and the belief that you are in a universe with a prime directive of:

**More Life for All – and Less for None**

*Steve McCurdy*
*Author of, The Whiteman Scenario*
*Houston, Texas*

# PREFACE

This book has its roots, as does everything I teach, in my own transformation, which began in the late 1980s. Everything about my life suddenly began changing rapidly for the better, including my income. I was, of course, delighted... but I didn't know *why* the change was occurring and I was convinced that it wasn't just "good luck" or that "my time had finally come."

Conventional wisdom wants to tell us large incomes are generated by attaining numerous degrees, climbing the corporate ladder, working harder and longer than everyone else, or playing the rules of the "game" better than everyone else. I was doing none of these things, yet my income doubled, then tripled, then went way beyond what it had ever been – into the seven-figure range.

I became intensely curious about what had happened, so I began to study. I figured somebody on the planet must know why these changes were happening and must be writing books or talking about it. Over the next seven years, I studied with some absolutely brilliant people who were able to explain the principles underlying what was happening to me. These underlying principles were, in fact, universal laws; laws as concrete and predictable as the law of gravity. These laws predict consequences of choices as reliably as the equations of acceleration predict the forces of gravity that helped us put a man on the moon and bring him back with astounding accuracy and safety. And, just as the laws of gravity were scorned until they were understood, the universal laws are often derided by those who do not understand them. But when your life is so dramatically and consistently changed, you cannot ignore the reality that SOME principle is at work. Understanding them can only help you better shape your actions and focus your choices toward your desired outcomes. Otherwise it is just "luck," and the universe is just too orderly to be explained that way.

I also realized that, because they are universal, these principles could be taught to anyone. Everything is affected by them… and nothing is not affected by them. As long as you are applying these principles, you *must* get the results they produce. If you drop a ball it always goes down and it doesn't matter who you are it still goes down. That is how the laws work. It's not different for different people – it works the same for everybody. So regardless of what you think or believe right now, you can have whatever you truly desire because that is the law.

I began teaching these concepts myself. I worked with companies and corporations, and eventually found that I loved working with entrepreneurs. For many years now, that's who I've been working with. I help entrepreneurs and solopreneurs to increase their incomes by learning more about predictably producing their outcomes. Entrepreneurs and solopreneurs have already taken the critical sorting step of deciding that their future is in their own hands. Many have come to the realization that the difference they make may not start with their great new idea or some slick plan, but is most affected by the higher, spiritual side of themselves. When you understand that the power to accomplish absolutely anything comes from changing *who you are being* rather that *what you are doing,* you can progress rapidly in whatever you want to do.

This material was originally a small introductory talk I used to present live called, "The Art of Success". In January 2007, I expanded it into a teleseminar. Those four, one-hour talks, which I made available in audio format on my website, www.davidneagle.com, provided the raw material for this book. I am glad to now offer these basic concepts about how to work with universal laws to create the life you want in easily accessible book format.

# CHAPTER ONE

## *Introduction*

When I was 6-years-old two years after a tragic fire took the lives of my uncle and two cousins I became aware that life was not going to be the same again. While my family struggled with how to deal with such a tragic life changing event I wondered why there was so much pain, suffering and dysfunction going on in my family and in the world. It was 1972 and the world was in a great state of stress change and then it hit me, the words that I would tuck away in my back pocket for the next 16 years until another event would cause me to take them out and look at them and begin to understand the profound meaning that they carried. "Does life really have to be this hard or is there simply something we as human beings don't understand?"

Growing up in a middle-class neighborhood in Chicago, then Phoenix, then Chicago again I saw that my family was not the only family to experience these difficulties in life. It seemed like every family that I witnessed was really struggling with some sort of problem and much of those problems seemed to be centered around a lack of money and then those problems expanded into many different areas. I also had seen people who didn't have money problems. I would ask various people in my life their opinion of why these people didn't have the same kind of money problems the rest of us had. I never got an answer that I thought was even close to the truth. Rather I got responses like "those people are lucky," or "different" or even "dishonest."

One thing I was pretty certain of was that luck didn't exist. I didn't believe that there was a "thing" called luck and that it arbitrarily landed in someone's life and that they then got to live a good, prosperous life. I also didn't believe that everyone who had money was dishonest.

Because... I didn't believe in luck... even back then. I reasoned that, "...if what happens in our lives is a matter of luck, then luck must be the operating force elsewhere in the universe. And nowhere do we see that happening."

My belief was supported by intuition, schooling, scholars, faith leaders and scientists all insisting that the universe functions in an orderly manner, and according to certain laws. The problem was that all of these disciplines disagreed about what the laws were or how they worked! My own logic led me to conclude that success must happen according to those laws also. And if it happens according to law, it shouldn't have to be difficult. Sorting out the law from everyone's different opinions… that might be the tough part.

I kept pondering these issues as I moved into adulthood, yet the solutions weren't coming. Very different schools of thought seemed to be able to use the same piece of evidence to prove their argument was the correct one. If these highly  educated, famous people disagreed on what was true how would I ever figure it out? I knew that there must be a foundational truth that governed everything and if I could find what was everything else would fall into place like the pieces of a puzzle.

One thing that helped me understand how we, as people, work (and that I will use throughout this book) is the "Stick Man" created by Dr. Thurman Fleet way back in 1934.

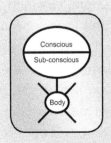

This rudimentary drawing divides the head into two parts and begins to explain how we think in accordance with our emotions and the actions we take as a result of the two. The two parts are the conscious mind (top of the head) and the unconscious mind (lower part). How these two act and interact produces the outcomes we face daily. You'll learn more of that as we move on but let's start first with the part we often think of as our reality or world that we experience and the results we have. At this point in my life I had gotten curious. And that curiosity led me to some very interesting places.

By the age of twenty-two I realized that I could very easily stay stuck exactly where I was my whole life! I was working as a forklift operator on a loading dock in Chicago, a high school dropout, recently married with two children. I worked six and a half days a week to earn about $20,000 per year, and I had no idea how to earn more than that.

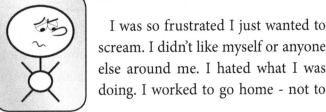

I was so frustrated I just wanted to scream. I didn't like myself or anyone else around me. I hated what I was doing. I worked to go home - not to do the good job that I was hired to do. However I knew that there must be more; that I was here for a reason. I just didn't know what that reason was. So I began to ask myself questions.

I began to ask myself, "What would I really like?" Now, here we'll start to look into my mind and see what is really going on behind the results that I was experiencing in my life up to this point.

I had never picked up a self-improvement book or anything of the sort, but I got out a little card and wrote on it what I wanted. The list was short: a boat, a house, a car, and $40,000 a year. I chose $40,000 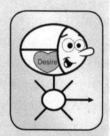 only because I had met a person who earned $40,000 a year, and at the time that sounded like it would really change everything for me because it was double what I was currently earning. In my mind I thought it would be the answer to changing my results. The key, I would later figure out, was that my desire was something I absolutely knew to be possible.

Did I want anything else? That was the sad part because when I would think about it I couldn't come up with anything else. Here I was, 22 with my whole life ahead of me and seemingly wanting so little. I had no idea why either and that seemed very strange to me.

In September of 1989, I had an accident that would forever change the course of my life although I didn't know it at the time. My son Joey was born in June of that year and like many babies, had a bit of colic which kept me up at night taking turns with my wife walking the floors trying to stop the incessant crying!! By September, we were exhausted and needed a much deserved break so we went and spent the day on my uncle's boat along with my parents. It was supposed to be a day of swimming, water skiing and relaxation but quickly turned into a fight for my life. After getting separated from the boat while I was trying to get my ski on I was swept into the swift current of the Illinois river at Marseilles and sucked through the dam.

It was an enormous wakeup call. A person could be having a grand old time in life or struggling in the depths of despair, it didn't really matter. At any moment, just like somebody flipped a light switch, that person could be *gone.*

We all hear that this is true but now I knew it really was true. We don't know when the transition of death will visit us but what we do know is that it will visit all of us at some point. It's our destiny from the time we are born.

After this brush with my mortality, I somehow expected everything to change. I wouldn't have to do anything. God was going to drop down out of the sky and say, "David, you've paid your dues. Here's your dream. Here  are the opportunities you need to accomplish it. You're all set."

I felt that I deserved success at this point, not realizing I had done NOTHING to deserve anything other than what I had. At this point in my life I had no understanding of the Law of Cause and Effect but that was to come soon enough.

But no dreams came true, no miraculous success dropped into my life. Nothing like that happened. I had broken my back. I lay around for a month while I was healing. Then I went back to work, as miserable and frustrated as ever.

One February night—I remember it was a Tuesday—I was working a forklift in the back of a trailer. It was about 2:20 A.M. and brutally cold outside. It had been a long shift, and nothing was going right. I was making mistake after mistake. Stacked cases of merchandise were falling over. I was exhausted and at my wits' end.

I broke down and cried right there in the trailer asking what is it I'm not doing right? How do I change this?

Suddenly a voice inside my head said, "David, change your attitude." The voice was so clear, it was almost audible.

I stopped what I was doing right there in the trailer. Could it be that simple?

Then that idea that I tucked away in my back pocket when I was 6-years-old came rushing in. The idea that it wasn't supposed to be difficult and I thought, "… could a small shift on the inside make a large shift in a person's experience on the outside?

Another little voice in my head was saying, "That's nonsense. Are you out of your mind? *Forget it.*"

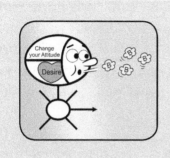

I brushed that voice aside. I wanted to think about this.

Those words, "Change your attitude," played in my head all the time I was running the forklift around on the dock that freezing Chicago night. Who did I know who had a good attitude, someone with a background like mine but living a very different life now?

The only person who came to mind was the owner of the company I worked for. This guy had a very large business, a worldwide food distributorship, and he seemed very happy. He dressed well and was pleasant to everyone. I knew he traveled a lot because the walls of his office were covered with pictures of the different places he had been with his family. I started to wonder, "What is it about this guy?"

I remembered the stories he told about how he had started in the same position I was currently working. I heard he started the business from his garage. How had I missed that? He was just like ME!! Not exactly though. He owned everything now and I still fought every second on that forklift and it was no secret to anyone I worked with or around. No one was offering me a promotion because I hated it… So, I thought, "He must have liked it at some level." Maybe that was the difference… He liked it at some level… while I despised it.

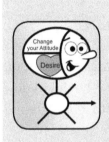

So I decided that was the first thing to change. "I don't love this… but I can act like I do. I am going to act as if I love what I am doing." I made that shift right there. I used my desire to consciously change my attitude.

What else was it about this guy? He treated everybody with total respect. I didn't. I was resentful. I was carrying mounds of emotional baggage from my past and as a result I was angry and didn't treat people with the respect they deserved. I decided I was going to start treating people with total respect.

There was something else. Loving what I did wasn't going to be enough. I also had to do a good job and change my reputation with the people I worked with and for. I realized that to build good business relationships, this man must have done every job to the best of his ability. My attitude was the opposite: "Let's get it done so we can get out of here." I was so damned angry, I didn't care if something was broken or placed the wrong way. They were paying me so little, I figured they deserved it. I thought, "That can only keep me where I am. So, I'm going to do every job to the best of my ability."

I didn't even know what my best was at that time in my life. I had to push myself and find out.

**Right where I was, sitting on that forklift, I decided to make those three changes. I was going to:**

1.  Act like I loved what I did,

2.  Treat everybody with total respect, and

3.  Do every job to the best of my ability.

**And I said, "You know something? I'm going to make a commitment to do these things for twelve months and see what happens."**

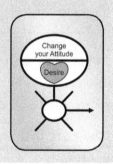

I really needed to learn what it meant to make a decision and stick to it.

That little voice in my head was saying, "No you're not. You've never in your life committed to anything. Every time you say you're going to change something, nothing happens. What makes you think you're going to do it now?"

I thought, "Boy, that's true." Even that feeling seemed to cloud my desire. All I could see for a second was that negative report card on my past record. But something had shifted. This time *I had to know.* I had to find out if what I had just understood could free me from being stuck and lead me somewhere had never been before. I said,

> **"I'm really going to do it this time. I am committing to make this change. *I believe this is the answer.*"**

What transpired in my life from that point forward most people would call a miracle. In less than twelve months I not only doubled – but *tripled* my income.

The part that was so bizarre to me was that the opportunity to do so was there right in front of me the whole time. I didn't have to wait or go searching for it. Once I made the decision to change my attitude and followed through everything began to change *instantly.*

Here is what I did NOT do:

- I did not go to school, or

- take any lessons, and

- I didn't read any books.

All I did was *shift what was going on inside my head,* and my income *tripled.*

If you had asked me at the time, "How are you suddenly making all this money?" To avoid further questions, I would have said, "I don't know. I guess I'm lucky," (despite my disbelief in luck.) My self-esteem was so low, I couldn't admit to anybody how I made the shift. I thought, "If I tell them, 'Oh, I just changed my attitude and it all began to happen'" they will think I'm nuts.

Even though I attributed it to "luck" when I spoke to others, I stayed committed in my *internal dialogue* to creating change in my attitude.

Even the people I worked with didn't understand how fast I was able to move up the ladder at the company I was now working for. People were still saying I was lucky or I was the part of the family that owned the company. You name it, they made up the stories. How can I blame them? My own mind was boggled.

I had spent my entire life losing and all of a sudden I was winning, consistently... and BIG. If I could think it, almost before I knew it, *it would happen.*

An interesting side-bar right here is that I did not know *how* I was doing this. I just knew it was ME and that it was connected in some way to this change in attitude. All of this explanation of the *how* came much later as I began to study how all of this works. The important point is, knowing *how* doesn't affect how well it works. Hold onto that. Because you are going to hear yourself asking "how" questions a lot. You've been asking it up to now. It is how the book got in your hands. You may ask it like I did when I got to this particular point in the story, because...

I actually got stuck at that point. I was earning $60,000 per year and wanted to get to $80,000, but I didn't know what was blocking me.

My mentor at the time asked me to consider a different idea: "Would I like to take that annual income of $60,000 and turn it into a monthly income?"

I said, "That would be great! How would I do it?"

He said, "No. Wrong question. Would you *like* to?"

"I would absolutely love to do that."

His response was, "Then you can."

Could my annual income really turn into my monthly income in a short period of time? As I began to play with the idea I realized it might be possible. I still didn't know how. But I also realized that, until I had become open to the idea, I had not believed it was possible.

Then he said something even more interesting. "You know something? It's actually easier to earn $60,000 a month than it is to earn $60,000 per year."

Sure enough. Within eleven months of making the decision to move to $60,000, I was earning $60,000 a month. Then we went for $100,000 a month. At that point, as clearly and dramatically as if somebody had lit a candle in a dark room, I became aware that earning money is one of the easiest things in the world. If it's not easy for you, you need to ask yourself –"why not?"

Since that time I've worked with thousands of people all over the globe, showing them how to unlock their potential. Success is your birthright. Your life should be abundant, prosperous, healthy, and full of love and friends. It should be absolutely amazing. If it's not, there's something you're not yet aware of.

I suggest that you give the material in this book some serious thought. It will do little good to read it once, put the book away somewhere, and forget about it. Go through the chapters frequently over an extended period of time until you have absorbed what they say and put them into practice.

If you're willing to do this, the life you dream of will begin to unfold right in front of your eyes. You'll think to yourself, "Where has all of this been all my life?" As Napoleon Hill wrote in *Think and Grow Rich:* "When riches begin to come, they come so quickly, in such great abundance, that one wonders where they have been hiding during all those lean years."

Why?

Because when your awareness shifts, you reach the tipping point, and change floods right in.

Shifting your awareness is one of the first things this book will teach you how to do.

# CHAPTER TWO

## *Understanding Who You Are*

Success is easily confused with achievement, riches, status, property... things. It can appear to be an elusive condition one must pursue instead of a state of being from which you must make your choices.

**The fact is: you were born to be a success.**

Now, that is a bold statement, but let's examine the evidence... and prove the point logically.

Who you *really are* can easily be confused with who you are *being* at any moment in time; how you are acting, what you are thinking and doing. The outward

17

evidence, your behavior, can be judged to *be* your identity—who you think you are. But that is a very limited view based upon a tiny piece of evidence. There is a lot more to consider when determining who you are. *You see people think they are their thoughts, their body and their results – and you are non of those things at all.*

Observation of the evidence available coupled with wisdom literature from all walks of life indicate that a principal underlying rule of the Universe… in fact, Rule #1… is MORE Life. The logical conclusion from that would be—You were born to *be* and *create* – **more:** more life, more opportunity, more money, more jobs, more houses, more laughter, more food, more trips to more places, have more ideas – create more life. If you study nature you see that all nature follows this rule and all nature has a purpose and it becomes that purpose. So, if the Universe's number one rule is MORE LIFE – then it follows that:

> **You were born with both a Purpose *and* the means to be a Success in that Purpose.**

In fact, the *only* way to stay stuck where you are is by buying into the idea that life and success are difficult and that they are something to be *achieved* rather than being something you need to *be*... Because you already *are!*

> ## Success is the constant progression of your Divine Purpose.

Because of the law – Rule 1 – you *will* manifest *more*. What you will manifest *more of* is the only question. Will it be more pain, more lack, more sickness, more allergies, more debt, more frustration, more traffic? If you're not getting the results you want in your life, there is simply something about Success and Rule Number One you do not understand.

There are two common misunderstandings about success:

- Misunderstanding Number One is that success lies in the future, that it is something to be achieved or a destination to reach.

- Misunderstanding Number Two is that success—whether in money, business, relationships, or any other area of life—is something a person needs to go out and get.

Both of these notions keep people looking for success in the wrong place.

Searching for something where it isn't leads to frustration and the wrong destination for your life. Your hopes and dreams fade, and eventually *you give up!*

Where, then, can this elusive thing called "success" be found? The answer will probably surprise you.

It is *in* you. And not at some future time. The success you want is in you – *already.* It is your divine birthright.

The fact that a successful life begins on the inside has been known for a long time. In ancient Greece, people seeking success in their lives would travel to Delphi to consult the oracle in the temple of Apollo. As they approached, they would read the famous maxim inscribed at the entrance: "Know thyself." And to "Know Thyself" you have to know where you came from. Throughout the centuries, philosophers and teachers have offered the same advice to their students.

No matter what you want, you can have it. I guarantee that you can have it, and I can show you how to get it. Because the great secret in life… which is no secret at all… is that you *already* have it.

How is this possible? Because of Universal Rule #1 (More Life), for all practical purposes, human potential is infinite. That is no small statement. To grasp its enormity, you first need to understand the significance of Universal Rule #1 – and of what that means about who and what you are.

## The Truth of Who You Are

Who are you? If somebody had asked me that question years ago, the conversation would have gone something like this:

"I'm David Neagle."

"No, that's your name. That's not who you are."

"Well then, I'm a man, and here's my body."

"No, that's the house you live in. 'Man' is your gender, but that's not who you are."

"Then who the heck am I?"

According to many spiritual traditions, a complete description of a human being includes all four of the following truths:

1. First and foremost, we are spiritual beings.

2. Second, we have emotions. The way we use the intellect we've been gifted with—the way we think, reason, question, and evaluate—governs our emotional state. One of the biggest problems people experience is being led around by their

emotions. In fact, they are conditioned to be led around by their emotions.

3. Third, each of us is gifted with an intellect, which means we have the ability to think and reason. No other life form on earth as far as we know, thinks and reasons to the degree we do. We're the highest life form of which we are aware.

4. Fourth and finally, we have physical bodies. We are spiritual beings living in physical bodies.

> **As fundamentally spiritual beings we are intimately connected to all the knowledge in the universe. Since spiritual energy has no limit, when we're working with that energy, we're working with infinite potential.**

Only rarely do any of us actually tap into that potential and put it to practical use in our lives. Yet *when we do,* what we can create is absolutely astounding.

## There is an Art to Success

When you understand what it means to be a spiritual being living in a human body and how this allows you to achieve the success you want effortlessly, then living life becomes like creating art.

What is art? Webster's dictionary defines art as "the conscious use of skill and imagination in the production of things of beauty." In this chapter and the chapters that follow, I will be teaching you the skills and describing how to use your imagination to create a beautiful life that reflects your highest purpose.

What do we mean by "success" in this book?

**Success is the constant Expression and Progression of your Divine Purpose.**

To my mind, what your heart truly desires to express in the world is, "your Divine Purpose." Increasing your ability to bring into being *exactly* what your heart truly desires, *exactly* when your heart desires it, is the optimal path to creating the life of your dreams; to creating success.

To bring this about, you will require energy and resources. While it is obvious that there are millions of resources surrounding you at all times, what most people live their entire lives without realizing is that the key to manifesting each of those resources are within you. Within the power of your purpose – a power that manifested you into being as a living, thinking, physical being holding this book – within that purpose is the power to manifest anything else from your reality necessary to fulfill that purpose.

Within you is the desire that manifests each of the resources that you will require: whether that is people joining their hearts and purpose with yours; or ideas that give birth to projects and jobs; trucks delivering your products world-wide; or merely the money to fund the next idea – all of it is within you at this moment. And it has been there since your purpose was conceived.

If this is true, why is it not apparent? Why don't we see the evidence of these millions within showing up without?

Excellent question. I will answer it with another question… If a door is locked yet behind that door lies everything you want and they key to that door is in a drawer how can you open the door? You can't until you take the key out and use it. It has no power sitting in the drawer only potential power.

Think about where you are right now in your life. What have you achieved? Are you satisfied with where you are? Would you like to go further? Does your income support the life you know you are meant to live? Are you choosing only those relationships that support the pursuit of your dreams? Are you living in an environment where you can thrive? Are you contributing your unique gifts to the world?

The Greek philosopher Plato said: "Life should be lived as play." Your life is meant to be like that. You can create every one of your days as a thing of beauty, spending your days with people you love, doing the things you love to do, and earning whatever amount of money you desire, to live however you choose to live. Life is a great journey once you learn how to live it as an art.

## Understanding Is the Key

Success is not difficult, but it does require understanding. By "understanding" I don't mean just knowing the ideas on an intellectual level. It would not be hard to read through this book, learn what it says, and fire it all right back at me. Some of what you read here you may have heard or read somewhere else, so you are thinking you already know it.

I tell people at my seminars, "I'm going to teach you a new four letter word that begins with the letter K. That word is, "Know."

People often say, "I know that. I've heard that before."

> "That's wonderful. Have you used it to change your life yet?"
>
> "Well, no."
>
> "Then you don't know it."

As Bruce Lee, the martial artist and actor said, "To *know* and not to *do,* is not to know."

If you say you know something but you're not taking the actions it implies, you have not yet understood it… OR, you don't believe it.

Oh, you may love the notion, embrace it eagerly, *wish* it were true with all of your heart – and yet – still not *believe* that it is true at your deepest levels.

Look back at Sticky. You were created as a Purpose – but all you could be aware of – both consciously and unconsciously – is your "Desire." It is subtle. And when, over time, all of those negative beliefs showed up around you, and were absorbed, they began to obscure your focus on your Desire. Even though you know the principles involved at an intellectual level, it is what you truly believe subconsciously that guides your choices over time.

What happens is your old fears and beliefs cloud that new *'knowledge'* that resonates so deeply with the core desire of your heart. In fact, you may have abundant life evidence that what you seem to *know*, and even have *seen* take place, isn't *always* the case. That creates a tiny seed of *doubt* that is reinforced by all the "failure evidence" your history has provided for you. The result is, you have this positive, useful information and you may embrace it eagerly, but you have it categorized in your intellect as a dream – a fairy tale. As long as this 'knowledge' is held in a 'wish it were true' place instead of a 'believe it is true' place... your results will support that level of practical disbelief.

What this means is, though you embrace the idea, you haven't yet absorbed the information, made it part of your belief system, applied it in your life, and *let it change you*. This is what I mean by understanding.

Unfortunately, our educational system doesn't teach people how to do this. They grow up with the idea that if they read something, remember it, and recite it back, then they "know" it. When it comes to achieving what you want in your life, nothing could be farther from the truth.

The Universe operates in an orderly manner, according to universal laws. To receive from the Universe what your heart desires requires *understanding* those laws and learning to operate within them. This means changing your beliefs, thoughts, feelings, and actions to align with these universal principles. As your understanding increases, confusion leaves, and you're able to make new choices that bring you totally different results.

I am often asked if embracing this perspective on Universal Law will conflict with a student's religious beliefs. My response is that these laws are described in the texts of almost every major religion on the planet:

"Hold faithfulness and sincerity as first principles."
—Confucius.

"Now faith is the *assurance* that what we
hope for will come about and the certainty
that what we cannot see exists."
—Book of Hebrews,
*The New Testament*

"The transmigration of life, takes place in one's
own mind. Let one therefore keep the mind pure,
for what a man thinks that he becomes:
this is a mystery of Eternity."
—Bhagavad-Gita.

And when Jesus said, "If you but had the faith of a mustard seed, you would be able to remove mountains," he was not speaking metaphorically.

The Talmud and Quran refer to the seat of this power as God or Allah but the principle is the same. The focus of this power is the expansion of life… More life.

It is also true that the interpretations of these writings – the individual dogmas – can serve to limit the power of the individual in applying these laws. But the underlying texts do not.

That is not to say that you will not be challenged to explore your beliefs more deeply. You will. Constantly. In fact, the limiting beliefs of those with whom you grew up will be the greatest block to your embracing, understanding, and implementing these laws in your life.

This is a *big* part of defining who you are. What you have been taught to believe is "impossible" or "not even real" limits your awareness of the truths in the world right around you. Truths that exist just beyond your fingertips – or your willing gaze.

Many of us were taught, "Don't ask questions," in these areas. How logical is that? What intelligent creator would limit the awareness of the creation unless it was for purposes of controlling and limiting that creation? And if the creator is creating with a purpose (and a primary directive/law) of ***More Life*** – how can that be served by limiting the co-creator's awareness? Don't waste creativity trying to justify an answer. The simple answer is: It can't.

Will expanding your awareness challenge your beliefs? Yes. Is it in conflict with the original teachings? It can seem to be... but upon examination and study, I have not found it to be. You must make that examination yourself. You must come to your own conclusions. BUT... if you come to the question with an open mind and critically examine the love behind the laws and the teachings of your religion, I believe you will find complete harmony... perhaps, even *clarity* on points that seemed odd to you before. I will go a bit further and say that upon a thorough examination of both, you can find them expressing the same idea.

There are no multiple truths. Truth is like the center of town. It doesn't matter from which direction you approach it... it is STILL the center... TRUE. It can be expressed in many ways... just as a multi-faceted gem will reflect different colors in different directions. But test what you think you believe for its TRUTH and I am convinced you will arrive at the same spot.

## Understanding Leads To Awareness

Understanding creates awareness. And awareness is a remarkable thing. So much potential lies locked up in every cell of our being, yet we can go through life unaware of how to use it or the gifts it could bring. You might be thinking, "I'd love to earn $1 million a year, but it's difficult given my current circumstances." It seems difficult to you only because you're not aware of how to do it. Said another way: it seems difficult to you because you believe your circumstances control your outcomes. If you were aware of a way to achieve your desired outcomes in the identical circumstances in which you currently find yourself, you would NOT believe it was difficult or impossible. You would KNOW it is not impossible. Nothing was ever more true than, "If she can do it… *anyone* can do it." If it is possible for one – it is possible for all.

Why, then do some seem to be able to do what others "can't." Because those that "do" are doing. Those that claim they "can't" are not making the choices necessary to move in that direction. Anyone "Can." Only some "Will."

Once you become *aware* of how to use the potential inside you, the results will absolutely blow your mind. Remember you already have this inside you right now!!

What do I mean by "awareness"? Let me explain with an example rather than a definition. As children, most of us think we learned how to ride a bike. Actually, what happened was, we became *aware* of how to ride a bike.

Think about this. Can you really teach somebody how to ride a bike? I don't think you can. You could write a book about it. You could write that little Mary (or Johnny) needs to get on the bike and put her hands on the handlebars, her feet on the pedals, and her backside on the seat. She needs to pedal forward while maintaining balance, and off she goes.

Well, after reading the book, or maybe having it read to her, Mary will get on the bike for the first time. We all know exactly what's going to happen. Mary and the bike will fall right over. We know that when it comes to riding a bike, intellectual knowledge is not only useless… it gets in the way.

What enables children to eventually ride a bike? They become *aware* of the balance that's already within them. The ability to ride the bike is not information little Mary and Johnny take in from the outside. They are born with the ability to balance. They just have to become aware of it.

It's the same with swimming. If you put someone in the water who is not aware of how to float, she is going to struggle, fuss, and fume. She is going to swallow water. Eventually, she's going to exhaust herself. She might even drown and die. Why? She thinks that she is not aware of how to float. She believes she *doesn't know how* and therefore, *can't.*

The truth is that each person already has the ability to float. To access it, he or she must get in the water and discover it. Even newborn babies are taught to discover their ability to float with simple exercises but if the parent is anxious or the temperature of the water is not ideal, or any number of other dissatisfying factors is present the infant may panic and begins to *believe* it is in trouble.

It may start to flail around and defeat its natural buoyancy. Many observing this imminent tragedy will scream, "Babies can't float!" But that is a wrong interpretation of evidence. It is not distressed because it cannot float – it is distressed because it is not happy with its circumstance and has a terrifying limiting belief.

If you have ever "had an idea," you should be absolutely clear on the fact that it just *showed up.* You may well have been thinking of other things or pondering in a different direction and then... suddenly... there was this idea. It might even have been only a partially formed idea but something about it was so attractive and interesting that you nudged it into consciousness and began to unfold it to see it more clearly. When this happened you didn't say, "I *learned* an idea today." What you more likely said was, "I *had* this amazing idea today."

Becoming aware is very different from learning. Learning is a matter of memory. When you're learning algebra, for instance, you have to remember the formulas and theorems. Once you pass the final test for the class you very likely never touch it again—until your own kids go to school. Then you try to remember, but you can't because you only *learned* a string of information… you never became *aware* of the principles of algebra.

Awareness is also more than "understanding." Mary, on the way to success at riding the bike, may go through a period of understanding—absorbing the technique, applying it, giving it her attention. She becomes aware of how to ride when that period of understanding and practice gives way to **surrendering to the capacity that's innate within her.**

Once you become aware of how to ride a bike or swim, that *awareness never leaves you.* You can stay away from the water or off the bike for twenty years. But get back in the water and you'll be able to swim right across the pool. Or get on the bike and you can take off down the road. Try that with a quadrilateral equation that you merely learned how to solve!

The same is true of awareness as it relates to success. Once you *understand who you are* and the abundant nature of the Universe and how to work with its laws, you never lose that awareness. Your circumstances may change, but you always have the ability to manifest whatever your heart desires most.

Think for just a moment about the idea of "confidence." Rather than provide the definition here I urge you to look it up on your own to see how well this idea of "confidence," sums up what we are talking about here. How much easier would living your life be if you were merely more *confident* that who you are is precisely what is needed in the next moment?

The definitions of confidence and faith have common elements that defy scientific measurement but are *more* influential in determining the outcome of any situation than the variables that *can* be measured. Some folks call these "intangible" qualities but I would say that *nothing* is more tangible than a person who has confidence in themselves and faith that what they want is what the Universe wants for them. In both cases – confidence and faith – the person possessing the quality has an unshakable awareness.

Faith and confidence in the Universe and its laws can be accepted pretty quickly. Accepting that what you truly *want* and are here to *do* will be supported by the Universe can be grasped as well.

But, knowing what your heart *truly* desires is a big question of its own.

In fact, once you become even marginally aware of who you are - no awareness will have more influence on outcomes than the certainty of knowing – *what you truly want.*

# Chapter Three

## *Discovering What You Really Want*

Note that the title of the chapter is *Discovering* – not *Deciding* – what you really **want.** While it is completely true that you will have to *decide* to go after what you want, what is even more true is that until you discover what you *truly* want, not much will happen. The decisions you make will falter when adversity is met if what you *think* you want is not aligned with what you *truly* want.

We make decisions based on the totality of our learnings and beliefs throughout our lifetime. Our decision process is based on all that data and some process that we have learned for picking a direction for our life from all of those mountains of information. Sadly, for the vast majority of human kind, the process is merely the "path of least resistance." The path to what you *truly* want is not likely to be the path of least resistance. It *can* be, once you are fully and completely aligned with it. But until then, every fear, false or limiting belief, and criticism you have ever met will raise itself between you and your goal to try to convince you to stay at the level of development where you find yourself now. Those fears will assail you with logical arguments to, "…set up camp here, at the edge of the frontier! Look how far you have come!!" And you may be only a shallow river crossing from your heart's deepest desire.

I would like you to step away from that for a second and think back to the things you thought you wanted as a kid. You didn't put limits on that, did you? You wanted to be a super-hero, an astronaut, a famous chef, a fireman/woman, a policeman/woman, a movie star – you wanted to be everything, and all things. But when you played… what did you "pretend" to be? Maybe that changed around among a wide variety of "roles," but who *were you* in those roles? That is one big clue to the true, deepest desire of your heart. The success you seek is in you. It was there *then!* Acting through *that* identity is "the way."

You are probably wondering: If success is already in me, where is it exactly? And how do I get to it? The answers to these questions require that you understand how your mind works.

Often when people hear the word "mind," they think of the brain. But the mind is not the brain. The brain is the physical organ or tool that you think with. The mind is not limited to a single physical organ. It is universal; that is, it is present in every cell of your body.

## The Mind's Dual Nature

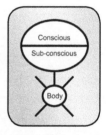

The mind consists of two very different parts. We have used our "stick man" from Dr. Thurman Fleet to show how these two parts of the mind interacted for me when I began my journey. Let's go more in depth here and learn how to use "Sticky" to understand our own internal experience, and to take the helm in steering the ship of our life onto the voyage of a lifetime.

The upper half of the head of Dr. Fleet's stick person represents the conscious mind, or intellect, the part of you that thinks and reasons. The conscious mind has the ability choose, so it's also where your free will resides. You hold the power to choose what you think, and nobody can take that away from you. No matter what you hear, read, or see, you can decide whether you want to reject it or accept it consciously.

The bottom half of the stick person's head represents the subconscious mind, also known as the emotional or "feeling" mind. Unlike the conscious mind, it has no power of choice. It retains *every* thought and feeling you have ever had and every idea you have ever been exposed to.

The lower circle in the diagram represents the physical body. This is the material medium in which you live and through which you express the contents of your conscious and unconscious mind.

The subconscious mind works like the hard drive of a computer. From the moment of your conception it is constantly fed information. This input starts well before the development of the conscious mind. At this point there are NO filters at all. EVERY experience is

recorded. The associations between an event and an outcome are dumped into the data record with equal weight and relationships between an event and a response get lumped together.

This happens even if the event and response had nothing to do with one another but just happened to be "taken in" at the same time or were "perceived" to be connected to another piece of information. Mark Twain observed this phenomenon when he said, "A cat won't sit on a hot stove twice... but he won't ever sit on a cold one, either."

Until our conscious mind develops, we program thousands upon thousands of bits of information *and form relationships between them* that may not have any relationship to truth. But we make most of our life decisions based on what we *believe* those relationships are.

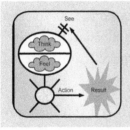

**Whatever is programmed into it is then expressed twenty-four hours a day as the emotions and actions that make up your personality and habits.**

From the top of the diagram... you have a sensory perception. In this case you SEE something, THINK about it and process that event through the FEELINGS. Then you direct your BODY to take an ACTION that produces a RESULT. You then SEE and THINK about the result, have a FEELING about and on and on. This happens with every stimulus in your world. If you don't give conscious, healthy expression to a thought or feeling, even if it is a negative feeling, you actively suppress it.

What gets suppressed will eventually express itself, but often in an unhealthy way as non-constructive actions, or even as illness. Certainly one of the most damaging aspects of these suppressed notions becoming expressed is that it will happen unconsciously, without your critical thinking and better judgment coming to bear. Like all of the actions you take, these unconscious actions will bring about corresponding results but you may not be aware or willing to believe you were involved, let alone were the one making the choices that brought about the results. Nevertheless, your choices and the responses determine the nature of your life. As you can see, then, what's going on in your subconscious mind is the key determinate of the external circumstances of your life.

If you ask them, most people will tell you that they wish their life were different. They wish they had more money. They wish they had better relationships. They wish they had better health. If they are entrepreneurs, they might wish they could grow their business or increase sales.

While they voice that wish, they are choosing it and holding it in their conscious mind. If they could focus on that wish for a long period of time, it would actually come into their lives. The fact that there is no external evidence of that outcome is also present. At that moment the subconscious has MORE evidence that the wished-for outcome does *not* exist than that it *does* or *could* exist. That "low score" from the subconscious creates a mental distraction from the vision created by the wish.

At this point an internal trial can occur in which the witness for the prosecution (the subconscious) challenges the wish to produce evidence of its reality. It can't. It hasn't arrived or been manifested in reality yet. It WOULD, if given focus and time… but the trial is *this minute!* So for many, once they take their attention off that thought, the subconscious steps back into control, causing them to again take the actions that perpetuate their current results – lack of the wished-for outcome.

This is the critical point at which the conscious mind COULD persist and take control. Most of this book will be about that moment. Certainly every outcome of your life will be about that moment. If the *limitations* of the subconscious mind define the choices that produce outcomes – then, what you will get is *more of what you have.* If the *possibilities* of the conscious mind define the choices that produce outcomes, then what you will get will be *new.*

This works the same way for everyone. Subconscious patterns block the person who is broke or burdened with debt from getting on his financial feet, just as they block someone currently making $10 million a year who wants to increase his income to $50 million.

The key to success, then, is to understand the subconscious mind and the *power of conscious decision*. You want to become aware of the subconscious mind's contents and what it is expressing in those in-between moments when your conscious mind is not in charge. You also want to find out *how to change* what's going on inside the subconscious that is preventing you from accomplishing what you want.

## Your Default Belief System

How does the information that's loaded into the subconscious get there? Much of it is picked up in early childhood. The stick drawing here represents an infant.

The top part of the mind, the conscious mind, is nonexistent, and the subconscious mind is wide open. The conscious mind doesn't fully develop until age seven. Until then, the child lacks the ability to reject some ideas and accept others.

Now, if you have ever experienced a two-year old you are fully aware that their favorite word is, "No." Close second is, "Mine." That would seem to indicate an ability to choose, and to an extent, it does. The little two-year-old mind has been filled with external data and has already made up some rules. These rules are based on *very limited* data sets and very unfocused filters. But, they are developing. "No" represents the build-up of an awareness of limits. "Mine" represents the build-up of identity. All of this, at 2! It will take another five years for that little mind to learn to function *critically* and begin to ask itself questions. In the meantime are *five years* of very emotionally charged data recording in that little sub-conscious mind.

All of the values, emotions, and opinions in the child's environment, including attitudes about money, business, sex, religion, and relationships, go right into the subconscious mind and become fixed in there. Around the age of seven, a cap is put on that wide-open mind, and from then on its contents are experienced subconsciously and are only challenged when the outcomes don't match expectations. At this age the matches are celebrated with joy and the mismatches with everything from withdrawal to tantrums.

The values, emotions, and opinions that you absorbed in your earliest years became your default belief system. Whether or not those beliefs served you, they began to be expressed in the way you thought, in your feelings about the events of your life, and in your responses to your circumstances. As you matured, other thoughts, feelings, and experiences were added to the contents of the subconscious to form your unique belief system and personality.

The key influencers in your life – your most valued teachers – built their belief systems in exactly the same way. They passed on to you what they considered the **best information** available to manage your life and development.

One of the great challenges of life is when an awareness begins to develop within you that conflicts with something in that core value/information set. It can be very upsetting when you begin to think, believe, and experience life differently from your core teachings. This conflict may be traumatic because the first ones will come when, as a child, you have very limited resources to act independently.

When things you have been taught, believe in, and have lots of experiential evidence for come in conflict with an opposing idea for which you consciously see real and validating evidence, you will be forced to challenge your core belief. We are told that the most painful experience for a mind is to hold two conflicting beliefs at the same time. The way most of us cope with this moment of crisis is to choose one over the other.

You may be forced to move from "I believe what I have been taught" to "Some of what I have been taught is not completely accurate."

At the deepest level everyone senses that there is only one truth. The spectrum of responses to a perception of conflicting ideas at this critical point in life range from throwing out everything you believe and starting over – to denying any information that challenges deeply held beliefs. Most of us fall somewhere in the middle and spend big chunks of our lives sorting out what is believed from what is true. How well we do this will show up either as life being hard… or as life being challenging but exciting and fun.

Think about how you were raised. What were the conversations like? Was there talk of not enough money? Did you learn that rich people were bad? Was working hard and long considered a virtue? What were the attitudes like with respect to success, to money, to relationships? Reflecting on the environment you grew up in will give you clues about the core assumptions buried in your subconscious; assumptions that, unchallenged, will control every decision and action you take for the rest of your life.

## Whose Beliefs Are They?

Whose values, attitudes, and emotions were these? Most likely they came from your parents or other people who had authority over you as a child. And where did they get their core assumptions? From *their* parents. And so it goes back through the generations.

I love an old story that illustrates this point very well. A newlywed couple is preparing their first Sunday dinner: pot roast. The bride is slicing the end off of the roast when the husband asks, "Why are you doing that?"

She replies, "Well, silly. That's how you cook a roast."

"Oh, ok. Well, why do you cut it off like that? Does it have to do with how slow or fast it cooks… or how the juices flow… or something?"

"I don't know… it's the way you do it."

"Oh. My mom didn't do it that way. Who taught you that?"

"My mom. Let's call her and see why we cut the end off."

The bride calls her mother and asks why she should cut the end off the roast before putting it in the pot. Her mother replies much the same way she had… "Well, Silly. That's how you cook a roast."

With her newly minted critical-thinking skills the bride pursues it, asking, "But, WHY? What does it do for the roast cooking part?"

"It is the way you do it, Hon. Your grandmother taught me."

With that the young woman decides to go to the source. She calls her grandmother and says, "Gee Gee. Hi! I'm making my first Sunday pot roast and I cut off the end and put it in the pot."

"That's right, baby. I hope it is delicious. You're a very good cook, you know."

"Thanks, Gee Gee, but my husband wants to know why you cut the end off the roast like that? How does that affect the way it cooks."

To which the grandmother replies, "Oh. I cut the end off 'cuz I don't have a pot big enough for a whole roast, Kitten. Won't fit otherwise."

Had the young husband not asked the question, who knows how many more generations of that family would be cutting the end off the roast and wasting good meat? I love this story because it is always good for a laugh… but, there are thousands of examples like this – in YOUR life – that aren't as innocent and that produce

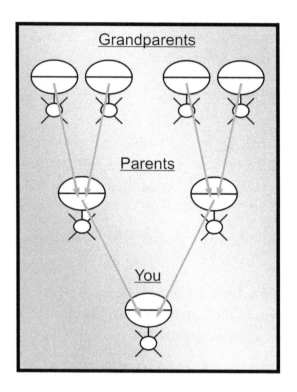

consequences far more impactful than a little wasted roast beef.

Again, let's use Dr. Fleet's tool, the stickman to illustrate this.

As adults, our grandparents made life choices and developed beliefs based on their own circumstances. In their subconscious minds, these mixed with the beliefs they received from *their* parents.

The grandparents handed these beliefs down without even thinking to their children—our future parents—who accepted them uncritically. These are taken as *truths* by their unconscious minds. Then they, dutifully handed them down to us, and we just accept them as, "the way things are."

Have you ever asked someone why they believe what they believe? Let's say someone tells you, "My religion is truth. It is the only way."

You might respond, "I completely respect that. But tell me, why do you believe your religion is the only way?"

"Because that's the way it is."

"And where did you get this information?"

The person might mention family, or name a certain preacher or a belief system.

You might then ask: "How do you know whether the information those people have is correct?" That might cause the person to think. It might also cause them to explode.

Deeply held (but unexamined) beliefs often carry with them a defense mechanism that lashes out at any challenge. This is rarely the case with beliefs that have been examined, tested, and consciously chosen. But beliefs that are deeply ingrained through tradition and family values can have taboos against being examined or challenged wired directly into them. To the extent any belief cannot stand up to examination, that belief will control the person holding the belief.

The founding fathers of America were pioneer critical thinkers. They held the new and radical belief that individuals had rights that were innate... not granted by a monarch... but rights granted by the natural order of things. This was earth-shattering thinking. Most of the present-day freedoms available in democracies worldwide were born in the minds of a tiny handful of these critical thinkers in a hot, humid hall in Philadelphia in the late 1700s. And yet, these men who stood at the forefront of critical thought in 1776 would be struck dumb by the site of a YouTube video playing on an iPhone. It would violate too many of their deeply held beliefs in what is possible. Remember, any technology that is beyond understanding is indistinguishable from magic. So, is it any wonder that something as personal and traditional in a family or culture as religion: the structure of beliefs in how *everything* works, would go unchallenged or unexamined?

Trust and loyalty are values that, if violated, create internal turmoil so great as to produce murder, mayhem and wars. That is how we react when our fundamental beliefs prove false. We *insist* that the truth we *know* remain *really* true.

Why can't we just "roll with the tide," if we discover some underlying belief is mistaken? Simple – if we were wrong about *that*... then what *can* we believe in? Must we now become responsible for examining *every* thought, rule, and belief we hold? Must we start over in life with no guiding star? Such a shaking of fundamental beliefs can strike fear into the most staunch among us. No wonder the argument is so often presented, "I know what I know... don't confuse me with facts!"

Well, that level of panic is also unnecessary. Our very existence is evidence that we are functioning in true alignment at many levels. But to operate beyond survival, to live out the desires of our hearts – we must be able to hold clean beliefs that are completely in alignment with how the universe truly functions. To do that, we have to unlearn anything that is not true.

I'm not suggesting that what you or anyone else believes is wrong. All I'm saying is: Have you ever thought critically about how you came to accept the beliefs you vehemently stand by? If what you believe is *true*... it will not be affected by your examination and understanding of it. Only the *false* disappears in the presence of light. And by that same token… only the *true* can endure in that light.

So for you to function at your highest level you must be dealing with rules you believe and understand. Those then become your tools for crafting a life that constantly moves you toward your desire and will do so much more effortlessly than you may be ready to believe. Think of it this way… is it easier to push a log up a river, or ride it down a river? Where you truly want to go is actually downriver from where you are… but it may not be downriver from the river you are on.

## Becoming Clear on
## What You Really Want

**Let's figure out who decided what you want?** Very often, *what we think we want* has been also handed down to us as part of the belief system we absorbed from our parents and other influential people while we were growing up.

A major reason why people don't create success in their lives is that their thoughts and actions aren't aligned with what they truly want. They are going after what other people want for them, or what other people told them they *should* want.

If you think about it, that's absolutely ridiculous. The results people are getting are not what they really want but all too often are driven by generational fears, insecurities, and ignorance. What's worse, the choices they make to try to correct those results are probably not their own either. Sadly, most people go through their life this way... and blame the Universe, God, Buddha, Jesus, Mohammed, their education, hairline, eye color, or family of origin. They never do battle with the real obstacle, which is trying to get to Philadelphia while dedicatedly committing themselves to staying on a train to Denver.

What, then, do you really want? I used to think: It would be a really twisted idea to put a human being here on the earth with no direction whatsoever. If the Universe is benevolent, then each of us must have some kind of a guiding system. Eventually, I was happy to learn that we do.

Each of us is born with a desire in our subconscious mind. What we call the subconscious mind the early Greeks referred to as the heart. This is the "heart of hearts" or the "desire of our hearts" that we hear about. As it says in Proverbs: "As a man thinketh in his heart, so is he."

We're meant to be taught how to identify that desire, embrace it, nurture it, and let it guide us throughout our life. Wallace Wattles, a pioneer thought-leader of success principles, put it like this: "Desire is the effort of the unexpressed possibility within that's seeking expression without through action." [ii]

> **Every other person and consciousness in the universe is ready to work with every other resource in the universe to move that possibility into reality with you.**

Now, Wattles is among my most revered teachers, and I find absolute distilled truth in his writing. The problem with distilled truth is that it is pregnant with meaning that requires study and contemplation to unpack. Let's see if I can do a little of that here.

What I hear him saying is, "You got here with a body, and a deeply planted internal possibility. That possibility is who you were sent to be. The yearning and desire you feel... the dissatisfaction, restlessness, and hunger... that's the part of you that *knows* about that possibility and will not rest until it is expressed in your life." I would add this bold assertion to that statement:

So with all of that power and drive available... what's up with these outcomes our lives are currently producing?

In the next figure, the heart shape in the unconscious represents your desire. "De-sire" in its root form means "of the Father" in the sense of being "of the divine." Here is an encouraging and maybe intimidating thought, but 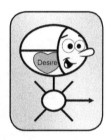 one in which I believe completely: At the moment of conception, a desire was placed into your heart. That desire is your true potential in *unexpressed* form. Its purpose is to guide you through your entire life.

Every choice you make, every direction you choose, every step you take will move you closer to or farther from realizing that potential. Now, here is the part that may seem counter-intuitive, particularly if you were raised believing that results only come from "hard work" – When you come into contact with that desire and align your decisions with it, incredible success will come with little effort.

Look how happy Sticky is when he is filled with just his Desire. He's moving toward it. Working "on your purpose" and aligned "with your Desire" you'll find you absolutely love doing whatever you do, and your days will be absolutely phenomenal.

Now… that is exceptionally good news. Search your own reaction to that idea. If you find yourself delighted, but doubting, scoffing, or even just a bit skeptical – NOTE THAT.

That "feeling" means you have a rule in place there. Somewhere in your rule system, you have an equation programmed into your emotional algebra that says "Hard, difficult, trying, challenging" = "desired outcome." This will absolutely guarantee that you will make choices in the direction of "Hard, difficult, trying, challenging." And if a little voice inside you is saying, "But wait… those are noble values," I would say, "Says who? Where did you learn that? Is that TRUE… or is it just *common?*" Here is an interesting test: ever done anything "Hard, difficult, trying, challenging" and have it NOT = "desired outcome"? I bet you have. Something is wrong with your rule if the math doesn't work every time, huh?

Well if the Universe is on your side… what is against you?

Every person has a heart's desire, but very few learn how to get to it. Why is that? When they look deep down inside their being, they don't see the desire. All they see are the beliefs they were handed by other people.

In this figure, the heart is barely visible behind all the little clouds of belief. These beliefs condition your conscious thoughts and desires. They express themselves through your physical body as feelings and actions, and you get the corresponding results.

You keep getting the same results over and over again.

Sticky isn't very happy here. Fear and limiting beliefs are masking his Desire. He is turning back to what he thinks he "knows."

You can't help going through your life expressing those unconscious beliefs. It happens automatically. Remember, you accepted much of this programming before you could even pretend to think critically.

Thomas Troward, an early teacher of mental science, says, "We cannot think into manifestation a different sort of life to that which we realize in ourselves. As Horace says, *nemo dat quod non habet*, we cannot give what we have not got." [iii]

By the time you reach for a book like this you have had a LOT of unexamined programming. The fact that you are reaching for the book and have made it this far is evidence that that desire is still showing through.

You may have an inkling of what your heart's desire is. But your beliefs tell your conscious mind that "...you can't do it. It's not right for you to do it. Who the heck are you to do it?" Such dysfunctional beliefs prevent you from thinking the way you would think if those beliefs got out of the way and your heart's desire could come to the surface.

In the Harrison Ford film, *Regarding Henry*, Ford's character, Henry Turner, is a heartless, ruthless businessman driven by the belief that the only way to win is at the expense of another. He is unaware that he is about to lose his wife, his child, possibly his business to this attitude. A traumatic head injury puts him into a coma and when he recovers he seems to be a different guy. He has forgotten everything including all of those values and must start over. In a particularly powerful scene his daughter teaches him to tie his shoes. "Where did you learn that?" he asks. "From you," she says. At his core he is open, child-like, eager to learn, hungry for connection. He has the mixed blessing of losing everything he had built and become to be left with just who he is and what he wants. It is a powerful example of how our beliefs shape our lives. We don't always get this dramatic a wake-up call. Fortunately we don't need one. All we need is to decide to turn toward our desire and then work to clear the garbage as it appears to us.

If you ask people: "How would you like to be financially independent and have as much money as you want to do with whatever you like? You could use it to improve the lives of others, to feed and clothe and educate people, and also spend it on yourself." Most of them would say, "Yes, that would be great."

Or you might ask: "How would you like to spend your days immersed in an activity you are so passionate about that you lose all track of time?" Most people would say, "Yes, I would love to do that."

We deserve to live that way. Not only that. We can live that way. And even more than that... we are *designed* to live that way.

Here is a point worth paying an incredible amount of attention to:

> **As a small child you were not responsible for what was loaded into your subconscious mind, but as an adult you are responsible for the contents of your subconscious... and what you do with it.**

This means that <u>you do not have the right to either assign that responsibility to others or to blame them.</u> It also means that <u>you can change what is held in your subconscious, and that you have the power to make that change.</u> You must make your own Declaration of Independence. You can connect with your heart's desire and release the false beliefs that do not serve you. In the coming chapters we will see just how to do this.

## Let Daydreams Be Your Guide

Human beings come into life not only with a guiding desire but also with the capacity to manifest it. As we saw in Chapter 1, any act of creation involves the conscious use of the imagination.

The first step toward the realization of that desire is to visualize, to imagine or dream about – what we want. But that capacity, too, is drummed out of us as we grow up.

When we're little kids, we have no trouble at all visualizing what we want to do. We can fantasize that we're astronauts or princesses, ballerinas or football players. If you give kids pots and pans and wooden spoons and keep them away from the television, they will create amazing things with their imagination. Nobody has to teach them how to do this. They're born with the ability to build images in their minds.

Once kids are in school, they're told that building castles in their imagination is not okay. To put a lot of children through a curriculum in a specific amount of time calls for conformity. When little Johnnie or little Mary starts to engage that wonderful imagination, the teacher says, "Get your head back over here. Pay attention to what you're doing." That could just as easily be translated: "Don't do what is calling you… do what I need you to do at this time."

As they get older, children are taught to replace that inclination to dream with "realism." Adults begin to ask, "What would you like to do with your life?" If they respond, "I would like to be a movie star," or "I would like to be a billionaire," or "I would like to save the world," the response is usually: "Oh, come on. You can't do that. You need to be realistic."

Well… as Robin Williams observed, "Reality… what a concept."

The message the fearful, "realistic" adult is sending amounts to saying, *"To become those things you are thinking about you would have to attempt, achieve, and pursue things I can no longer imagine. I cannot cope with the idea that you get to do what you want to do when I have suppressed that belief in myself. So, since you trust me, I will pass down to you the lie I bought into to keep things simple and falsely secure."*

The trap continues. As they're finishing up high school or college the question becomes more pointed: "How are you going to earn a living?" Very often, they don't know. They look outside themselves, to parents or teachers or even peers, for direction. They're told: "You seem to show an aptitude for this or that. Based on economic and business trends, you might fit very well right *here.* You can become an engineer, or a secretary, or a truck driver." All of this is based on a presupposition that being who they are and pursuing that direction would not bring with it the means of survival. This is a presumption of lack. This kind of doubt-planting is so subtle that it rarely is challenged, but plants a deep and powerful seed of connection between the person's dream and fear of not having enough.

What are we asking these young people to do? Based on limited information from other people, they're supposed to make a decision that will affect the rest of their life. Whether they become an engineer, a doctor, or a truck driver determines their income, where they'll live, who they'll associate with, the quality of the clothes they'll wear, where their kids will go to school, the quality of their healthcare, where or even if they'll take vacations, the quality of their retirement, the kind of cars they drive, the restaurants they go to, what they give for gifts on holidays, and more. Yet they're asked to make that one decision at an immature stage of life with very little information about their own potential.

How often is a young person asked, "What is the desire in your heart? How can we help you bring that to the surface, express it, hone it, discipline it, and then earn with it whatever amount of money you need to live the lifestyle you want to live?"

As an adult you can correct this. You can set yourself free. You can get in touch with your heart's desire and realign your purpose with it. You can also retrieve your capacity to visualize and dream. When you do, it's like the gates open and everything you want starts flooding in. No matter where you are, no matter what you are doing, you can accomplish anything you want, you can be whatever you want. And it doesn't have to be difficult.

## Identifying Your Heart's Desire

The chapters that follow will show you how to realign your life's purpose with your heart's greatest desire. But you must begin by first uncovering this desire. Before you move on to the next chapter, take some time—at least a week—to consider and complete the following exercise:

Ask yourself two questions. These questions are simple, but the answers are often buried deep within you and sometimes difficult to uncover. The first and most important question is:

What does your heart desire above all else? Once you have the answer, write it down.

> **"What do I want?"**

Then ask yourself the second question:

> **"Why do I want it?"**

Why do you believe your heart desires this? I urge you to take your time with this. Search deeply. Is your desire for this object, achievement, or experience felt beyond all logic and reason? Does it seem to be deeply connected to your life's purpose? Or is it because you were told at some point in your life that you should work towards having this? Or perhaps you believe that other people who have this object, achievement, or experience are happier than you are?

Let me be crystal clear about something. There is no more important question to ask or answer to pursue than the clear and focused idea of what it is you truly want. As you ask this question and as answers present themselves you will mature in your ability to be aware. With that will come clarity about how you answered the question. It will become refined and ever more in focus. It is possible you will discover that you originally thought – with all your mind – that you wanted X, but you are now coming to discover it is really Y or Z that you want. Be grateful. Do not despair that your original answer was not precise. It got you to the clarification didn't it? It helped you find TRUE didn't it? Then it was *perfect!* Celebrate it. Choose. Find the answer. What do you WANT??? That is always and forever the most important question and take the answer to specifics – to six decimal places!

The second question is meant to help you to identify a false desire; one that is not aligned with your life's purpose but one you've been carrying around with you because at some point you "learned" that you should want it. Ask the question. Test it for authenticity. If it turns out to be a false desire, then permit yourself to release it. I will talk more about release in a moment… but first:

Return to the first question. Go deeper this time, meditate upon the question: "What do I want?" When a new answer comes, ask the second question again: "Why do I want it?"

Continue until you arrive at a want that is purely heartcentered and purpose-filled. This is your heart's desire as you understand it at this level of awareness.

Once you have uncovered it, you can't lose it among the clouds of belief again. But you want to clear away the false beliefs as much as possible so your desire can shine through, and replace the false and limiting beliefs with beliefs that support the expression of your desire.

This is the topic of Chapter 4. But before we go there, let's look at this business of "release" for a second.

This journey to your heart's desire will reveal to you, over time, many instances where you have derailed yourself or allowed yourself to be derailed from your primary journey. This can produce feelings of guilt, shame, anger, and blame. None of them are useful or true. They are distractions produced by more old habits and untrue teachings. Rather than engage in any form of negative energy, celebrate the discovery of this truth. The prior-held belief that no longer serves you was useful to you in achieving some outcome. It took you in a specific direction and helped you produce the results of the life you have led up to now. Be grateful for this discovery and for the learnings that this prior journey has equipped you with. You may never have gotten to this place without them. But, now that they are no longer useful in getting you to the *next* point on your journey, you can release them with your gratitude and love. Harboring continued resentment for them will keep you there.

On this business of finding your true heart's desire, I would direct you to the principles of artillery fire. Surprise! Artillery is huge guns that fire projectiles miles away at targets that the shooters themselves may not be able to see. Tables and calculations have been devised over the years that can help the firing officer determine which way to point the muzzle of the gun, what angle to elevate it to, how to account for the winds here, in transit, and over the target... for they may all be different, and so on. But no matter how much math she does, the artillery officer can only expect the first shot to tell her what the gun is currently aimed at... (where she IS).

So... she fires. And something on the other end blows up. The fire control officer on that end looks through the binoculars and says, "Great shot. You are 300 yards short of the target and 150 yards to the East."

Now our firing officer needs to adjust the gun. She needs to turn the gun to the West four "clicks" on the adjustment and 9 "clicks" higher so the projectile will go a little farther. She makes the adjustments. And she fires. And over the hill... something else gets hit.

Miles away the fire control officer sees the second shot impact. "Okay… we're still a little east but the distance is perfect."

"How far east?" our shooter asks.

"You came about 80% of the way. Adjust it west by about a quarter of what you did last time."

So the first shot showed her what she was aiming at and the second calibrated the gun's adjustments. Two more clicks to the west and this time she should hit the target.

Now, I tell you that ballistics story to ask you some questions. Did the shooting officer or the fire control officer have ANY frustration or guilt over missing the first two shots?

No.

Of course not. They were finding out what they were aiming at and how the gun worked. By the third shot they should have sufficient data to hit the target. So the lesson here is that, in artillery, the first two shots don't count. And I contend that your first few shots at identifying your heart's desire may be off a bit but each will give you valuable information about which way you are off and by how much.

# CHAPTER FOUR

*Letting Go of*
*Unwanted Beliefs*

I n the diagram below, Sticky is "stuck" in a terrible loop. Like many of us, Sticky has grown up with some limiting or negative belief. As she moves out

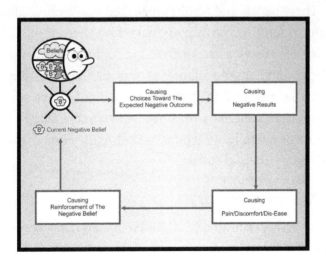

into the world she will unconsciously make choices that move toward those expected negative outcomes. Not surprisingly, it will produce negative results, which will cause pain and reinforce the belief. Until Sticky changes the belief… the results will keep working out this way.

The beliefs that we carry in our subconscious mind – true or untrue, good or bad, limiting or empowering – largely dictate the choices we make. The choices we make produce our present results. The present results are judged as "good" or "bad" (also according to ingrained beliefs) and that all combines to determine our life circumstances.

These beliefs and results are locked into a cause-and-effect loop that our friend Sticky finds herself in. This cycle of causation can keep us stuck or move us forward, depending on the nature of our thoughts, feelings, actions, and beliefs. Though we certainly have some conscious awareness of those beliefs, more often and more powerfully, we tend to verbalize the combination of these beliefs as stories.

## The Power of Story

Fearlessly examining your present results is an excellent place to start in discovering what you truly believe. (What did we hit with that shot?) When you examine your present results—where your business is now, where your finances are now, how much you're earning, what your relationships are like, the state of your health—it causes you to think. That is, you may *think* that you're thinking—that you're being rational and objective—but in most cases, that's not all that's going on. You're also *reacting*. That is, the subconscious is also at work, conditioning you to see your present results a certain way, which prompts a certain emotion. Past the age of 7, these cycles become automatic and, for the most part, well outside of your conscious awareness. But by purposefully paying attention to "what comes up" you can start to see the patterns and cycles your story has generated in you.

For instance, someone might say the word "airplane." If you once had an experience on an airplane that scared you out of your mind, you will have built an association between the concept and word "airplane" and will experience the negative emotions. The reaction can be instant and profoundly "real" in your experience. The fear, anxiety, and worry will appear with the mere mention of the idea of an airplane. It works the other way, too. You may have had only wonderful experiences with airplanes. When you hear "airplane," you think, "Education. I can travel to new places, explore, and have wonderful experiences." Along with those thoughts you automatically experience emotions of happiness, excitement, and anticipation. That one word can elicit either set of emotions, depending solely on the contents of your subconscious.

The day-to-day results you produce in your life stimulate emotions in much the same way. Based on how you are conditioned, what you see creates a thought, and that thought creates an emotion. Unless you decide to behave otherwise and interrupt the pattern, you will be deep into the emotional experience and may never examine what triggered it.

What happens after the emotion? You go right into your story. What is your story?

> **Your story is the excuse or explanation you have created around a result.**

Very often it's the reason why you believe you can or can't do something. It usually describes your subconscious beliefs and wraps them in an explanation of why you behave the way you do and justifies the choice as logical and right "given the circumstances."

You might say, "This happened because. . ." "I can do this because. . ." or "I can't do that because. . . ." You have bought into the story. Very often the story is not true.

As we saw in Chapter 2, it's not necessarily even your own story. It may be the story of your grandmother who had a small roasting pan!

Don Miguel Ruiz, a shaman of the Toltec tradition, wrote about this in *The Voice of Knowledge:*

> *Before I was born in this physical body, a whole society of storytellers was already here. The story was ongoing. From their story, I learned how to create my own. The storytellers who are here before us teach us how to be human.*
>
> *First, they tell us what we are—a boy or a girl—then they tell us who we are, and who we should be or shouldn't be. They teach us how to be a proper woman, a decent woman, a strong man, a brave man.*
>
> *They give us a name, an identity, and they tell us the role that we are playing in their story. They prepare us to live in a human jungle, to compete with one another, to control one another, to impose our will, to fight against our own kind.*
>
> *Of course I believed what the storytellers told me. Why wouldn't I believe them? They filled me with knowledge, and I used that*

*knowledge to copy their style and create my
art in a similar way.* [iv]

Ruiz makes a statement and asks a question so obvious that it might get overlooked. He says, "Of course I believed what the storytellers told me. Why wouldn't I believe them?" What a powerful question!! As children we know that we *"don't know"* and are happily guided by these masters around us who function powerfully in the mystery that is our tiny world. Why *wouldn't* we trust and believe them? But, then a day comes when what they have taught and the reality we are experiencing diverge… and we are in a pickle.

At our center we are beings that understand emotional algebra long before we learn the math in school. We learn to trust/distrust, believe/not believe based on evidence and associations throughout our lifetimes. From the moment we meet our mother's eyes while nursing we begin to form associations and the building blocks of beliefs. We take two pieces of evidence, "I am warm and fed," and, "Mom is here." Then we make a logical but mathematically inaccurate equation (assumption), "Those must be equal. Mom = warm, fed… safe."

The energy of teenage rebellion is fuelled, not by some cosmic shake-up in our biology (though that amplifies *everything*) it is fuelled by the awareness that the people we learned to trust implicitly... our childhood guardians, our parents, grandparents, teachers, family... have the capacity to be *wrong*.

This challenge to our primary safety association/ belief causes a conflict between the conscious and the unconscious. That is a crisis. Always. We are thrown into a turmoil that has been written about since the cave. It becomes the model for how we deal with those conflicts between belief and any awareness of contrary evidence. It becomes our story. And unless we own that and decide how we "choose" to believe, it will *remain* our story.

Your stories, then, are what stop you from taking action on your heart's desire. Your heart may be saying: "I would love to start a business," "I would love to multiply my income," "I would love to travel," "I would love to meet that great woman or that great guy" . . . "but I can't." Why not? Then comes the story.

As our "Stuck" Sticky diagram shows, the story influences your actions. When you tell a limiting story, you are letting it keep you right where you are. That story is reflecting back to you, and to anyone you tell it to, exactly what you believe.

## The Power of Belief

Beliefs, whether inherited unconsciously as a small child or carefully chosen and trained into us over time, are powerful. Think about this for a moment. Throughout human history right up to the present, groups of people have been at war with each other. If we examine why, the reason—the story they give—*always* comes down to a difference in their belief systems.

The United States is the first country created by a blend of beliefs. Much of the conflict in our internal history comes from the clash in belief systems between groups of immigrants. Even in a more evolved and tolerant United States where there is a wider belief in "live and let live" there are still life and death struggles *daily* that boil down to a difference in what two people hold as true. It seems that is not enough for a belief to "work" for a given group. In many cases the belief requires the believer to convert or kill anyone holding a different belief. Terrorism could not exist without this "belief." It has been said that the human brain has two functions: to keep you alive, and to keep you "right." In a healthy, mature brain that is the proper order. But history is filled with stories of persons who chose to be *right* even if it cost them their lives.

If a belief is powerful enough to cause people to kill or sacrifice their lives, we'd better take a look at the beliefs controlling our income, our health, our relationships, and life circumstances, because they are just as strong.

The power of belief can be harnessed for good or for evil. Consider Adolf Hitler, for instance. Imagine that somebody comes over to your house, knocks on the door, and says, "I want to come in for a cup of coffee. I have a phenomenal idea." The two of you sit at the kitchen table over coffee, and he leans across the table and says: "We're going to create a world of one-race people." "Really? Okay. How do you plan to do that?" "First, we're going to burn the books. Then we're going to burn the people."

You'd think, "*This guy is out of his mind.*" But Hitler got a whole nation of people believing what he believed. How? He had the ability to instill his belief in others.

On the other hand, many people have used belief to achieve great accomplishments. Take the Wright brothers as an example. They believed they could invent a heavier-than-air machine that could fly, and they persisted in their belief through repeated failures. The flight at Kitty Hawk on December 17, 1903 moved their belief into reality, and history.

They did it. They flew. They even repeated the feat. It was a recorded *fact*. But beliefs are powerful things. Five years after Orville and Wilbur got their airplane off the ground there were scientists in Europe who still believed it couldn't be done! The Wrights said, "What do you mean, it can't be done? We've had the thing in the air for five years. You can't say it can't be done. We're doing it."

Beliefs are the engine – the power plant that drives your decisions, choices, actions, and the results and outcomes in your life. They either keep you from getting where you want to go, or they are the sails that carry you there. If your life lacks purpose and you don't feel excited about what you're doing, it may be because what you *believe* you want or "should" want for your life isn't truly what your heart desires. Or you might have a driving hunger to do something absolutely incredible with your life, but inherited false beliefs are holding you back.

The life you lead will be the product of what you believe.

> **The first law of the Universe is "More Life" – and you *will*, by design, manifest *more* of whatever kind of life it is your unconscious mind deeply believes.**

If there is a conflict between what your conscious mind *wants* to believe and what your unconscious mind *does* believe you will live in the product of that conflict. And since your conscious mind sleeps and your unconscious mind does not… the predominant evidence in your life will be manifested from the most deeply held and reinforced belief.

By that same rule, beliefs aligned with your heart's desire have an equally powerful force to propel you forward. Obviously, then, understanding how to discard the beliefs that are not serving you and replace them with beliefs aligned with your heart's desire is critical if you are seeking a change in your results. This change is not the product of some herculean effort on your part; it is the product of a change of mind. Change your internal reality and, as Sticky's feedback loop on the first page of this chapter demonstrates, your results will change *automatically*.

## Take Responsibility for Your Beliefs

How do you let go of the beliefs that are holding you back? This is particularly challenging when you consider that you may have no idea what those underlying beliefs are. One might assume that a deep course in unpacking all of your mental history might unveil the source of those beliefs. And, while such a route can be very enlightening, there is a more direct route.

By accepting personal responsibility for those beliefs, as well as for what they cause and what causes them, you can cut through the fog and begin *immediately* to restructure your internal rule system. *This is the magic key* that unlocks the door to success. If you want to change your results and achieve higher levels of success, accepting complete responsibility for your life and every choice and consequence in it is a commitment you will want to renew to yourself every day.

You begin by taking responsibility for all your beliefs, and along with them, accept responsibility for every thought you think, every feeling or emotion you experience, the perpetuation of your story, every action you take, and every result in your life.

Think of it this way: You wake up one day to find yourself at the yoke of an airplane headed straight for a mountain side and spiraling down at a steep angle. The ground is rushing at you at a dizzying speed. You can wonder how you got there or you can reach out, take the yoke and point that plane away from the danger. It really doesn't matter that you think you don't know how to fly. And it really doesn't matter how you got there. The *only* thing that matters in the next moment is you accepting responsibility for flying that plane out of the death spiral. In fact, taking time to think, lay blame, find the cause… all of that will guarantee you will crash. The *only* hope for escape from the crisis is for you to take responsibility and take control. Will you make mistakes? Guaranteed. Will you learn from them? That too, is something for which you must accept responsibility.

If you are to live a life of your own choosing, you must accept responsibility for every thought, feeling, belief, action and result you experience.

***Responsibility for every thought and feeling.*** "Every" means taking responsibility for all of your thoughts and feelings, including the negative ones. This can be a challenge when at first the responsibility doesn't seem to be yours. For example, someone may be rude to you. You respond inside with an angry thought. Your feelings are offended. The natural response is to blame that person for what you're thinking and feeling. Your story might be: "He (or she) *made* me think and feel this way."

No, *you* made you feel that way. Note that the experience of being offended isn't occurring in the other person. It's happening in you. They merely made a "choice." It is *you* who are "taking offense."

No one really has the power to offend anyone else. The soft spot is inside the receiver. To illustrate: If a woman is talking to a man who has a lifelong weight problem and she tells him, "You're fat," his feelings may likely be hurt. If she says the same thing to a thin man who has never had a weight problem, he won't be offended. In fact, he will probably think *she* is the one with a problem. Why? He doesn't have the same psychological sensitivity.

***Responsibility for every belief.*** As a child you passively accepted the beliefs that were handed to you. But as an adult, you have the capacity to accept responsibility for every belief you hold, expressed as the stories you tell yourself. You do not have to remain a victim of your inherited beliefs. You can choose which ones you want to hold on to (there may be some good ones, like: the Universe is benevolent, or generosity is a virtue) and let go of the ones that don't represent what you want for your life or the truth of who you are.

You can say, for example: "I accept that I inherited the belief that money is hard to come by from my parents, because they struggled. But I no longer choose to be a victim of that story."

***Responsibility for every action.*** If you take an action that turns out to be a mistake, accept full responsibility for it. For instance, if you responded with a nasty comment to the person who was rude, acknowledge to yourself that you engaged in action that at some level you regret. You might even decide to apologize.

One reason people don't like to take responsibility for their mistakes is that as kids, they were told they were wrong for the mistakes they made. They were made fun of, or perhaps were corrected with anger instead of compassion. But addressing a mistake should not be about punishment. It should be about helping the person understand his or her mistake so he or she won't make it again.

We're often the ones who are hardest on ourselves. But beating yourself up over something that went wrong only perpetuates your making more mistakes. Instead, wake up in the morning, look at yourself in the mirror, kiss yourself, and say, "I'm a wonderful human being. I deserve the best. And I deserve to give the best." That positive attitude has its roots in taking responsibility for all of your thoughts, feelings, stories, and actions.

***Responsibility for every result.*** Finally, take responsibility for every result you experience, whether positive or negative, whether in business or your personal life. This is actually an empowering stance. If you don't accept responsibility for your results, you're putting that responsibility on someone else. Then, in order for your situation to improve, somebody else has to change. You have handed power over your life to someone else.

I like to equate this kind of awareness to the planned mid-course corrections NASA schedules into every mission. At various points in the flight the position of the craft will be compared to the planned or desired position. In rare instances they are right "on course" but more often some kind of corrective burn is needed to return to the desired flight path. While both NASA and the onboard astronauts accept responsibility for getting back on course, no one goes through "guilt angst" that they require this change of path. They note it, make the correction, check that they are, in fact, back on course, and the mission continues. If the variance from course is outside the tolerance of the expected drift, an examination into the underlying cause of this gap in calculations will be undertaken, but not in order to lay blame. Rather, they are seeking to identify this unknown vector of force, in our case a deeply held belief, which put them in an unexpected place. Once identified and accounted for they can plan to counter that force next time. Again... no "guilt angst"—just the acceptance of responsibility for where they found themselves and how to avoid that in the future.

## Release Limiting Beliefs

As you take responsibility for all of your beliefs and the cause-and-effect loop they create, you become aware of the ones that are negative, limiting, or false. These no longer represent your highest good and your heart's desire.

Name these falsehoods for what they are; recognize them as part of your old programming. *Be grateful for them.* They belong to the past, and your past prepared you to become who you are now. However, they are no longer needed. You can release them.

How do you release a limiting thought or belief? By expressing it. It's not wrong to express something negative because that was your experience. Expressing it may even be the catalyst that takes you to the next level. But it needs to be expressed in a healthy and safe way.

Whatever you don't express, you suppress. What is suppressed will eventually express itself through you in an unhealthy way, and you are likely to keep repeating it over and over again. This can even cause "disease," which is simply a condition of the body when it's not "at ease."

One simple form of healthy expression is to write out your unwanted thoughts on a piece of paper while letting yourself experience whatever emotions go with them.

What needs to be let go of will come out on the paper. Take that paper and burn it while you forgive everyone and everything you wrote about. Just let it all go.

Another form is forgiveness. Make forgiveness a daily practice. Forget about what another person might have done in the past that impacted you. Release every person, situation, and circumstance to the highest good and move forward.

Above all, forgive yourself. None of us is perfect. We've all done stupid things in the past. And I have news for you: You'll do stupid things in the future. You can't change what has happened, so you might as well let it go.

Many people tell me, "How can I forgive this or that situation? You just don't understand." Of course, I understand. I went through the same struggles. It isn't easy. It isn't hard either... it is tricky. We have lifetimes of subtle, intricate training that we have accepted and *practiced* that are deeply rooted in our belief systems. We are not consciously aware of the choices we have made that are now in place in our unconscious mind as life *rules*. Unwrapping those cords, establishing new, more supportive beliefs requires *awareness* of these rules and a conscious decision to take another direction. I have walked *hundreds* of people to this place and watched and supported them as they have faced the seemingly insurmountable challenge of re-wiring their unconscious minds. I can say without hesitation that I do understand. I can also assure you that there is one and only one way for the conscious mind to win out in a contest with the unconscious mind on a matter of life rules.

**First, accept responsibility.** Even for the most challenging situation. Realize that you attracted it for your growth.

**Second, practice gratitude for it.** Understand that whatever is taking place is a result that you've created. An undesirable result is simply a sign that you're going in the wrong direction and you need to make a course correction. Remember NASA? Make the course correction *without* guilt and shame.

If you don't shift into gratitude, you remain resentful. And if you are resentful it will be difficult to release those thoughts and feelings, and nothing will change. Resentment produces terrible internal feelings and the simplest way to avoid that is to not think about them: denial. If facing these issues is associated with feelings of fear, resentment, anger, and pain you will avoid thinking about them and won't have a chance to look for the needed course correction.

If, however, you look at this awareness with gratitude – not as an attempt to *trick* your subconscious – but if you *truly* realize what an enormous gift it is to have a signal that alerts you to an internal rule that is not supporting you – everything has a chance to change. If you express gratitude for discovering this rule which exerts profound force on your choices – choices which directly dictate your results – if you can *truly* see how lucky you are to have found that key, you can then begin to make the adjustments necessary. Gratefully embrace the adjustment you must make to release that faithful, though misguided, guardian of your choices. Then move as an aware adult into decisions which take you toward the desires of your heart without guilt, shame, or resentment.

The best book I know of on the topic of responsibility and gratitude is *As a Man Thinketh* by James Allen. Don't just read through this book. Study it, absorb what it says, and practice it… gratefully.

## Replace Old Beliefs with New Ones

As you retire unwanted beliefs and the thoughts, feelings, stories, and the actions they generate, you can replace them with others that are aligned with your heart's desire. Going forward, you can commit to making all your decisions based upon your newly upgraded beliefs.

You can say, for example: "I let go of the belief that money is hard to come by. Instead, I believe that money is abundant and accessible to me, and that I always get what I need when I need it." Let this become your new story about money.

Align your thoughts and feelings with the beliefs that support you in achieving your heart's desire, and take the actions that represent these beliefs. Those new beliefs will produce different actions. Different actions will bring new, more desirable results.

Then as new awarenesses of limiting beliefs emerge, you can wash, rinse, and repeat.

# CHAPTER FIVE

## *Identifying Hidden Motivators*

Beliefs, whether ones that are handed down to us or ones we choose to align with, come with underlying presumptions about ourselves and the nature of the world. Limiting beliefs tend to be based in assumptions that we are in a state of need or lack. Extended, these beliefs produce the idea that we are insufficient, inadequate; require care and tending, etc. Hitler proved that the best way to sell a lie of this magnitude was to mix as much truth as possible into the story and link the truth to the lie.

It is true that as small children we are dependent on the adults around us and so we truly are in a state of need. But ideally we grow out of this as we mature. When we do *not* grow out of it, those needs can remain as hidden motivators that shape and drive our choices.

These too can be examined and addressed to help loosen the hold of any beliefs we want to let go of. To quote the ad executive, "Makes sense, if you don't think about it." So… let's think about it and remove its hold on us.

## Schindler's Six Needs

A number of years ago I came across a book called *How to Live 365 Days a Year* by Dr. John Schindler.[v] In the book he points out that every human being has six basic needs:

The need for love

The need for security

The need for self-esteem

The need for creative expression

The need for new experiences

The need for recognition

Basically, the list is a variation on Abraham Maslow's famous Hierarchy of Needs, which was introduced in the early 1940s. A lot of thought-leaders continue to use Maslow's list today, putting their own twist on it.

At first glance, the list made complete sense—these are six things every human being needs. However, as I thought more about it, something about the list did not sit right with me.

At the time, I was teaching sales and recruiting, and I kept noticing a peculiar phenomenon. I could give two people the same kinds of leads, the same sales copy, and the same marketing strategy. One would get phenomenal results, while the other wouldn't.

What was happening with the second person? Most probably it had a lot to do with what was going on inside: something was affecting that person's decisions and actions. As James Allen writes in *As a Man Thinketh:* "We think in secret and it comes to pass, environment is but our looking glass." Since I was thinking about the list of needs, it occurred to me that trying to get one or more of these needs met might be getting in the way of my students' marketing practices.

Trying to *get* something from outside ourselves is evidence that we believe we don't already have it. We believe we need it, and that we have to get it from someone else. Then the decisions we make and the actions we take become driven by a hidden motivation to get that thing. This brings poor results.

You see, the laws of the Universe don't bend. And one of these universal laws is that in order to *get* you have to *give*. If we're always trying to get a need met, then what are we giving? Nothing. We're being needy, and we're not really giving.

## False Needs Become Hidden Motivators

I asked myself: What if the six things Dr. Schindler identified weren't really needs? Curious to see what would happen, I took out the word "need," and was left with a simple list:

*Love*
*Security*
*Self-Esteem*
*Creative Expression*
*New Experiences*
*Recognition*

I immediately noticed something about these six: the first three are internal, the second three are external. As spiritual beings connected to limitless Source, the first three we naturally have already. To assume we need them is ignorance.

The second three involve engaging with the world around us. Creative expression occurs in and impacts our environment—we make a contribution to the lives of others, create a piece of art, write a book, create a business or a new product. New experiences involve exploring outside the limits of what is familiar. Recognition is something we give to others and also receive from them. So I arranged these six in two sets:

| Love | Creative Expression |
| Security | New Experiences |
| Self-Esteem | Recognition |

Then I noticed something else: the first three are the keys to the second three. This insight, I realized, was more than a word game or semantics. This realization has the power to transform absolutely everything in a person's life.

If your belief system is based on the assumption that Love, Security, and Self-Esteem are things you don't have, you will look for them *outside yourself.* They will operate subconsciously as *hidden motivators,* quietly driving your choices. Your decisions and your actions will be aligned with getting these supposed needs met, rather than with your greatest good. And most frustrating of all… you'll be looking in the wrong place!

This is what was happening with some of my sales and recruiting students, and it happens all the time. Business is just one good example.

## How Hidden Motivators
## Undermine Our Choices

When a business fails, whether it is a major corporation or an entrepreneurship, it doesn't happen overnight. It happens over time because of a series of wrong decisions made by the owner or manager. Very often those wrong decisions are driven by an unrecognized need for Love, Security, or Self-Esteem.

A lot of people operate their business with the unconscious motivation of getting Love. They make choices to create a good feeling with a client because, beyond wanting their client's business, they want the client to *like them*. When it comes to nuts-and-bolts matters, like asking for money or talking about sales, if the interaction isn't warm and friendly, they feel an emotional disconnect from the client. Then, in order to win the client's good opinion again, they devalue themselves: they don't charge what they should be charging; they don't raise their prices when they should, and so on. And the very natural result is: the business fails.

A perceived need for Security can be equally insidious when it comes to business. Though the numbers vary across industries and sources, it is generally estimated that over 80 percent of businesses "fail" within the first year. The business experts will tell you it's because those businesses were undercapitalized. No. The only way a business can fail is if you quit. The number one reason businesses fail is because of fears around Security and *thus not taking the right risk at the right time – and not being able to get yourself to do what is necessary when you need to.*

For example, an entrepreneur might receive an offer to go to a seminar that's perfect for developing his business. Yet he will say, "I can't go because I can't afford it." Are you kidding? He can't *not* afford it. He attracted the opportunity into his life. Now he's saying, "I can't go; I don't have the money" instead of saying, "Wait a minute. This came into my life for a reason. I *have* to do this. My business needs this in order to grow."

The Law of Polarity says there can't be a right without a left. There can't be a question without the answer. Similarly, an opportunity cannot appear in a person's life without the means to make use of that opportunity being available as well.

What prevents us from thinking this way?

Take this page in your hand. If you are reading on an e-book, pick up a piece of paper. Do this physically so your mind has a chance to accept it. You are looking at this type or the page facing you. Let's call that the "front." Now turn the page or flip the paper over and look at what we call the "back" of the page, then come back here.

Did you do it? The "back" only exists because of this "front." True? If this front were NOT here… there could be no "back." Correct?

Everything in the universe works this way and we understand this as the Law of Polarity. If something exists… its opposite exists. Dark and light are the very easiest of concepts to exemplify this law.

You must come to the conclusion in your heart of hearts that this is true to master the art of manifesting. Think of it for just a second… this gives enormous power to every perceived frustration in your life. Now, instead of a perceived need for a resource being frustrating, it is *the very evidence you need that it exists!!* You would not have thought of it otherwise.

Once this truth penetrates to the level of *belief,* you will move from frustration to focus. You will be able to take undesired outcomes and use them as feedback, like NASA's mid-course correction "fix" taking. You will know where you ARE. And as we have amply proven, knowing where you are is fully half of getting to where you wish to be.

The frustration that comes up from meeting an unexpected outcome is a *false feeling*. This false feeling is based on a hidden motivator for feeling "Secure." So... letting the desire for Security serve as a *hidden motivator* instead of recognizing Security as something we already have causes us to misinterpret the outcomes (which we are producing) *as negatives* instead of what they truly are; evidence of where we are.

Self-esteem is similar to Love as a hidden motivator, in that both create a need to get something from another person.

What people with low self-esteem are seeking is approval. Somebody always has to give them a pat on the back. How does low self-esteem show up in business? When entrepreneurs buy into the idea that they are competing against other entrepreneurs for new business, they worry about their ability to secure a sufficient share of the market. However, if they trust *and demand* their inherent ability to attract the perfect clients and accept that they fill a unique niche just by being themselves, they'll have no lack of business.

## The Truth about Love, Security, and Self-Esteem

It is said, "Know the truth, and the truth shall set you free."[vi] The truth is that, as a spiritual being living in a physical body, you are always connected with Source.

> **You were born with access to all the Love, Security, and Self-Esteem you'll ever need.**

Your true nature is Love. And if you *are* Love, you don't need to *get* Love from someone else. In fact, you can give Love unconditionally because you are yourself powered by a limitless Love.

True Security has nothing to do with becoming a multibillionaire. Somebody could make a mistake with your money, and it could be gone tomorrow. Real Security lies in knowing how to create wealth because you understand the *Laws of the Universe*. If you know how to create wealth, and if you believe in your innate ability to create what you want when you want it, you have that Security for the rest of your life.

What is interesting to consider here is – you *already* are creating what you need when you need it. Let me say that one more time – you are creating what you need, when you need it.

You may be thinking, "But I don't exactly know how to create wealth whenever I want." Don't worry. I'll tell you more about that in the remaining chapters of this book. Start with the understanding that – the resources you need are within you.

***The Millions Within*** refers to this fountain of resources that were wired into you at conception. Most people, when they see that title think "Millions" of dollars. And while there is no limit to the money you can make when you are aligned with Universal Law, The Millions Within refers to ALL of the resources at your disposal.

Most of these assets – resources – will manifest as true Security, Love, and Self-Esteem… and some of those will manifest as dollars. If need be, many millions of dollars.

Finally, the truth about Self-Esteem is that as a spiritual being tapped into the limitless potential of the Universe, you can create anything that you want. There is nothing you cannot do or become – because you already *are*.

Understanding that you already have available to you all the Love, Security, and Self-Esteem you'll ever need, you are free to engage in the other three elements on Dr. Schindler's list: to express yourself creatively, to embrace new experiences without fear of loss, and to give and receive recognition to and from others. In fact, the second set of three will manifest effortlessly in your life if you base all your decisions and actions on the belief that you already have the first three in limitless quantity.

Greatness is present in every person, but to recognize it in others begins with recognizing it in yourself. Those who say they see the greatness in somebody else but do not yet see their own may be quietly envious of the other person because at a deep level they're still trying to get recognition. Once you see the greatness in yourself, however, you can't help but see it in somebody else.

Feel proud of yourself. Remind yourself of how wonderful you are. You don't need validation from anybody else. You are great by being who you are right now.

## Six Affirmations

Going forward, how can you train yourself to make decisions free of the influence of hidden motivators? I recommend that you begin by changing all six of Dr. Schindler's needs into affirmations. These are statements that you'll want to say to yourself on a regular basis.

*I am love.*
*I have security.*
*I have healthy self-esteem.*
*I freely and creatively express myself.*
*I create new experiences.*
*I recognize the greatness in myself and the greatness in others.*

You can declare these six affirmations as the underlying principles of a business or a great relationship or anything else you want to create. If you do, you will find that the endeavor, whatever it is, becomes not about *getting* but about *giving*. You will not be able to help but give, because that's who you *are*.

Everything that you give out comes back to you. You must release any internal message that tells you otherwise. That's the law. Action and reaction are equal and opposite, and energy always returns to its source of origination. If you send out love and good ideas to other people and look for how you can help everyone you come in contact with, your relationships will be great, or you'll have so much business you won't know what to do with it all. Whatever you choose to do, it will be successful when it comes *from* abundance and in the spirit of making *More Life To All*.

## The Three Keys to Self Acceptance –
## (Which Lead to Self-Confidence)

When you know without question that your source of Love, Security, and Self-esteem is your own spiritual connection to the Universe, you grow in confidence. The more you understand yourself and who you really are, the more confidence you develop.

There are three keys to having extraordinary confidence.

- First, know that there is only one source of supply. This means that everything in the universe comes from one initial source. Everything that comes from this source must come through various channels of distribution or delivery, i.e. money and opportunity come through other people but from the one original source.

- Second, think, speak, and act only positively about yourself. Never refer to yourself, your circumstances, what you do, or how you feel or think in a way that does not represent the person you want to be.

- Third, surround yourself only with people who support *your purpose and your dreams and respect how special you really are.* Another way of saying this is: don't spend time with people who do not believe there's something wonderful about themselves. Why is that? Because if they don't think they are wonderful, they won't see the wonderfulness in you. They may tell you they do, but they don't. They cannot give something they don't have. Instead, they're subconsciously trying to get something from you.

## Identifying Your Hidden Motivators

Here is an exercise to help you become aware of your hidden motivators: Keep a personal notepad or voice recorder with you. As you go through your day, keep track. Ask yourself:

- Why am I making this decision this way?

- Why am I saying yes or no to that?

- Am I trying to get love *from* another person?

- Am I afraid of losing my sense of security?

- Am I afraid of rejection (the flip side of love and security)?

- Do I find I am talking about myself in critical, unflattering terms?

When it comes to finances, ask yourself:

- Why am I making the decisions that I am making.

- Am I afraid I will fail or lose an opportunity or spend too much money?

- Am I afraid to step out and do something I've always wanted to do because somebody might not approve?

Start paying close attention. ***Get this stuff down on paper*** so you can look at it closely. You cannot change anything of which you are not aware.

I recommend that you commit to this exercise for no less than twenty-one days. Very likely you will find that one hidden motivator is more prevalent for you than the others. Record a brief comment on how this hidden motivator is affecting your life now. Note also how it may have affected your life up to this point.

This information lets you know where to focus your internal work so you can immediately begin making decisions that support your success.

> **Pay attention – Become Aware.**
>
> **You cannot change anything of which you are not aware.**

## CHAPTER SIX

*Knowing Where You Are –*
*and Where You Are Going*

So far, we have seen that the key to accessing and employing the Millions Within involves:

- Remembering your spiritual connection to the Universe, (Source!)

- Identifying your true heart's desire,

- Replacing limiting beliefs with ones that support the expression of that desire, and

- Addressing hidden needs that may deflect you from what you really want.

This work is personal and intimate. It takes commitment, a certain amount of internal skill, and an overwhelming desire to live your best life NOW.

Once this internal part of the work is underway, you are ready to manifest in the physical what in the past you only dreamed about. The first step on *that* journey is to identify where you are starting.

When you want to travel from one place on the planet to another, what do you do? You determine where you are now (for example, in your house in a certain town in America). You choose exactly where you want to go (for example, a certain beach on the Mexican Riviera). Next, you get clear about the relationship between the two. Then you can decide how to move from one to the other. (As a little aside here I would remind you of our NASA mid-course correction. The astronauts have no guilt or remorse about where they are. How they got there isn't a factor. Where they *are* and where they *want to be* are the only considerations. Likewise, you don't need to waste any energy guilting or shaming over where you are with respect to your goal. It is where you are! Only by seeing that clearly will any of the next steps be relevant and work.)

When it comes to achieving what you *really* want, you must start with a clear understanding of where you are. However, this is the point where many people become stuck. They don't take the time to become clear about what they really want to create in this life.

And—just as important—they don't put enough attention on where they are right now.

## Becoming Clear on Where You Are

The need to become clear on where you are surprises a lot of people. It's perfectly natural to assume that where you are is obvious and jump immediately to where you want to go: I need more money. I need more time. I need a different relationship.

You too may be thinking, "Come on, you have to be kidding. I know exactly where I am."

Do you?

If you try to jumpstart from where you *think* you are, instead of from where you *actually* are, you will be starting from the wrong place. Suppose I blindfolded you and drove you out into the countryside, dropped you off without telling you where you were, removed the blindfold, handed you a roadmap, and told you to make your way home. You would know where home was, but because you wouldn't know where you were starting from, you could walk around forever trying to find the correct route. Someone would have to tell you where you are and from there, how to get where you want to go.

What might stop you from asking for directions is ego, pride, thinking you know the route – maybe you don't want to look stupid or vulnerable. These are the same factors that stop people from taking an honest look at where they are. You have to be honest with yourself, even if you don't like your present situation and don't want to analyze it. Put your pride and ego away. You can tell anyone else whatever you like, but you can't run from yourself.

## Assessing Your Level of Awareness

You are probably wondering: Know where I am in what terms? The answer is: In terms of your level of awareness. And the best indicator of your level of awareness is your present results. (It's true: your present results let you know what your subconscious beliefs are, as we saw earlier; they also are the measure of your level of awareness when it comes to achieving what you want. What you are producing is what you are aware of and what the total of your energy is focused on. If you are most aware of disappointment and fatigue… that is the result you will see. If you are most aware of opportunities, excitement, "magically" appearing relationships with "coincidental" synergies… then *that* is what will be produced.)

Take any aspect of your life: your relationships, your income, your savings, the opportunities offered to you, the size of your client base if you're in business. The results you are experiencing are based on your current level of awareness in that area of life. For instance: What is the most income you've ever made in any twelve-month period? Whatever that amount may be, whether $20,000 a year or $60,000 a year, that is the amount you are currently aware of being able to generate in that time frame.

To take your income to the next level is a matter of developing the awareness appropriate to the next level. When you change your awareness—when you change your *belief about what is possible*—the situation is able to simply transform.

Yes, it's possible to move from one level to another through hard work. You may say, "I worked long and sacrificed to get where I am. I'm a self-made woman (or man)." That's a worthy achievement, but do you want to continue to live that way? People spend all their life struggling and striving because that's what they have been taught, but it's not the only possibility. You can also up-level your awareness and get where you want to go relatively easily.

You don't learn how to ride a bike. The ability to ride the bike is within you, and you simply uncover the awareness of it. Similarly, you already have the ability to earn whatever amount of money you can imagine, but you have to bring the corresponding new level of awareness up from within. The current awareness of the person who is earning $20,000 a year is set for earning $20,000. Could she earn $100,000 or $1 million? Absolutely. Without question. It's actually easier to earn those large amounts than it is to earn the $20,000, but she is not yet aware of how to do that.

## Envisioning Where You Want to Go

Once you have determined where you are *now,* you can turn your attention to becoming clear about where you want to *go.* Just to say, for instance, "I would like to have a million dollars," or "I would like to have an infinite source of income and be independently wealthy" is not clear and specific enough. This is where the use of conscious imagination comes in.

If you want to set an income goal, sit down in a quiet moment and connect with your heart's desire. Make the decision to believe in magic if only for this exercise, and ask yourself: "What do I want my life to look like twelve months from today?"

Begin to imagine it in detail. Write down exactly what house you would like to live in, the mortgage that comes with it, the utility bill, property and income taxes, health insurance, what car you would like to drive, what vacations you would like to take, what investments you would like to make, what amount you would like to tithe; make a thorough and comprehensive budget of the resources needed to live the life you are picturing. Then go on the internet and find out exactly what each of these would cost in today's dollars. Add all of the figures up, and there you have your twelve-month income goal.

When you first start to write down what you want, your brain will try to flip over and ask, "How are you going to do that?" Since you can't think of how it's going to happen, you might tell yourself to modify what you want to something more reasonable. Don't do the exercise this way. Instead, do it assuming you cannot fail. Be like a kid before Christmas, or as if you are standing with Aladdin's lamp in your hands before a genie: No matter what you ask for, you are going to get it.

Your goals—the financial goal or goals in any other aspect of your life—need to be connected with your heart's desire. It also needs to be in specific terms. And it works best if it has a specified time frame.

## "How" is Not the Question

Now that you know where you are and where you're going, you are ready to see the difference between them. Take a piece of lined paper, or take a piece of blank paper and draw six or eight horizontal lines across it. These lines represent different levels of awareness. In truth, there are millions of levels of awareness, but the few lines on the paper are enough to represent them. As illustrated in the next figure, in the lower left-hand corner on the bottom line, write down your best-ever annual income. In the upper right-hand corner, on the top line, write the word "goal" and an equal sign and then put down the 12-month income goal you would like to achieve.

This diagram can work for any goal in any area of life—health, relationships—not just money or business. However, let's say your goal, based on your research into where you want to go, is $1 million twelve months from now.

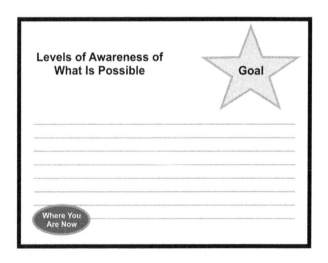

As soon as you choose and write down that goal, what's your next thought? For most people, as I just said, it is, "How? How do I get from here to there?" If that's the first thought that comes to your mind, just consider it useful information about your current level of *awareness*. The hard-to-grasp truth is, *you don't have to know how.*

You might be thinking: "What do you mean? We've been taught that we have to know *how*. That's the next thought: How? How do I bring in that money?"

No. It's the wrong question. The question to come back with, the question that will actually produce results for you is:

"Where am I?"

You are where you are in your life right now—you are at the level of awareness attached to your current results. There's no shame in this. Remember the mid-course correction idea? As a matter of fact, you should have a lot of pride in it. You can congratulate yourself and be grateful for being where you are presently, because from here you can move to where you want to be next.

## The Way Change Happens

***Once you understand where you are, a shift occurs inside you.*** You become able to see the next step that can move you forward. Resources and opportunities appear that guide you further up the path. A favorite example of mine is the idea of driving from LA to New York and driving *only at night*. It is a great metaphor for how we function in life, actually. Driving at night, in the dark with only a clear idea of your ultimate destination, it becomes crystal clear that knowing where you are is *critical*. I hear you saying, "But I need a MAP. I need a HOW!" Well, what you get in this life is a direction – an intention. Then the *journey* gives you feedback all along the way. Your headlights only light 100 feet of the pavement ahead of you. But with good, sound *direction* and a clear view of the next 100 feet, you can drive right across America at night and end up in Times Square a few days later. Will you take a few detours? Probably. Will you have to backtrack around some dead-ends. Very likely. Will you get there? You will, ONLY if you keep going in the direction of the goal.

It sounds a little crazy, but I assure you, this is the way it is. There's an old saying, "When the student is ready, the teacher will appear." That's absolutely true. When your awareness increases, the lessons and road signs that were there all along become visible and understandable to you.

How does this happen? When you are honest about *where you truly are* and bring light to your situation (those headlights shining brightly on where you *are*), you flip yourself into a different vibration, meaning a different level of awareness. All of a sudden a new possibility—an opportunity—is revealed (the next 100 feet). You see the next step, which on our diagram is represented by the line above where you are now.

You don't see how to go from your best annual income all the way to the $1 million on an interstate super-highway. You see the next step... and maybe the step after that. But that's usually about it. The thing is... that is enough.

The next step always comes as an inspiration or opportunity to take a specific action. You have to *do* something, like make a certain phone call. Or in a business setting, your next step may be to hire an assistant. The specific action, then, would be to shift your business model or budget so you can bring the assistant on board.

As an example, imagine yourself standing at the bottom of a long flight of stairs. The only way to get to the top is through a series of continued actions. You lift one foot and place it on the stair just above the one you're standing on. Then you apply pressure and lift yourself up. Each time you do this, you don't know for certain what the outcome will be. You might slip. The step may be weak and give way. You might arrive on the next stair safely. This means you have to move forward in faith. Does that mean you risk something? Yes, absolutely. If you want the reward, you're going to have to risk. If you're afraid to take the risk, you will stay in the same place. That's the law.

Infants know this. You were an infant once, weren't you? Babies have *no idea* "how" to operate the body they are in. But they can see something they want and they keep trying things until they can crawl, then walk, then run in the direction of their interest. They tend to fall down a lot. They skin their knees sometimes. What they don't seem to do is *stop*. They keep going until they get there. Ask any parent of a toddler and they will tell you in no uncertain terms that the desire of a child is simply unstoppable. That has not changed since you learned to walk. The rules of the Universe worked for you then and can work for you now. But you have to be aware of what you want, where it is, where you are… and not stop.

<u>Once the next step is revealed, you must accept that it is *truly* your next step.</u>

This acceptance is the second internal change that takes place—the first being to develop awareness of where you really are. If you don't accept this opportunity, the only option is to reject it. If you reject it, you stay where you are. If you stay where you are, you'll start asking the question "How?" again. Then you'll lead yourself around in a circle like a dog chasing his tail. So if the new action that's presenting itself will move you toward your goal, it's best to accept it. You will note in our example that babies spend almost no time in analysis. They seem to be about forward moving action. Good tip!

Taking that next step requires you to change a third time: to change your beliefs about what is possible for you to achieve. The baby, blissfully, never gave the first thought to limits. It wants... so it *goes*.

You can't tell somebody how to do this any more than you can tell her how to float in the water. The person has to experience it. To discover how to float, she has to stop panicking and flailing around and begin to relax—that is, begin to change her belief structure about what she is capable of. The nature of this change is determined by the nature of each next step. Here's the key: The next step is usually outside of your current experience - but not out of your reach.

Here is a critical point that I could not mention before walking you through this whole process. In reality, changing your belief about what you can achieve—for instance, that you can receive $1 million in twelve months—is the very first internal change you must make before you begin applying this exercise to your life.

> **You must accept the new belief that you are capable of acquiring that amount of abundance.**

Then the steps that allow you to make that a physical reality will be revealed one after another through the months.

Most people think they resist change—though that's not really true. What people really resist is *being* changed. When the change is their choice, they usually accept it pretty easily. *Eagerly* in many cases.

You change—you go up a level in awareness. You adapt to the change. And then you grow and change again. It's a metamorphosis. As you embrace the next step and then the next, each time adopting an upgrade of your belief system, you mature. Another petal of you opens up. You unfold like a flower and blossom.

You repeat this process all the way until you get the goal. But let's remove the word "get." Some people say we "achieve" the goal. I don't like that word either. The word that works best is "receive." Through this process, you *receive* the goal. Since the goal is something you're in harmony with, the seed of it is already inside you. All you have to do is *be* it. You unfold and then you receive it. It just comes into your life.

## A Word of Warning

As you step into these new realms of awareness, like our toddler, you will enter a world that may not have been "toddler proofed" for you. Just as you unconsciously make a thousand compensations as you walk and run as an adult, you had to learn the necessity for those as a new "mobile" person. You learned it from hard knocks in most cases. That will be true here as well. You will meet resistance in the form of new territory, new rules of which you are not completely aware as yet. You will learn… and learning always involves paying the price of *attention*.

In addition to the challenges of new territory, you also will discover dozens, maybe hundreds of latent beliefs that will rise up to keep you at that lower level of awareness. Your unconscious beliefs will scream at you to "go back!" It may manifest as headaches, stomach trouble, seemingly unmotivated anger… lots of ways. This is a critical moment for you. You will, in all likelihood, have to make a very conscious decision - <u>What will you chose to believe?</u>

The old limiting beliefs will try to convince you that Rule One – More Life – has a border… a limit. *"Come on. Be realistic," "Who do you think you are?" "WE don't do that kind of thing."* – and on and on. You will have to decide whether or not Rule One – More Life – is actually true, or if in all of the Universe, since the dawn of creation, YOU are the exception: for YOU, and only for you, there are limits to the abundance of your life.

This is the wall that has kept you where you are. If you persist you will discover that it is *not* a wall. Like a haunted house at Halloween, it is an illusion that is very convincing, and very scary – but that cannot truly hurt or limit you. Here's the shocker… you built it. Others handed you the bricks and mortar, but you built this illusory wall by believing in its reality. It serves you, in fact. It keeps you safely housed at the level where you are. At this level you know how to cope with all of the challenges. The evidence for that is that you are still alive. You *know* you can function at this level, because you are. Everything you want and dream about, the desires and passions of your heart, are on a road on which you are currently standing… but the road seems to run under this *wall*.

The temptation is to dismantle the wall through conscious understanding of every brick. That takes a lot of time. That isn't how you've overcome obstacles before. As an infant eager to become a toddler you did not wait until you understood the mind-muscle connection in your legs. You just *went*. You probably *still* don't know "how" you stand up. But you do it. This can work that way too. Don't try to out-think it. Act.

Nike was right; Just do it.

## The Exponential Rewards of Change

When you shift to a new level of awareness, you don't just discover the ability that helped you to get there. _Everything_ on that plane of awareness becomes available to you. Much of it will be concepts you never considered or imagined. Bonus! No extra charge. The Universe is abundant that way.

When you became aware of how to ride a bike as a kid, a new kingdom opened up for you. Now you could engage in activities with your friends who had also become aware of how to ride a bike. You could go to new places, go farther, get there faster, and usually stay longer because getting home took less time than when you had to walk.

You could race bikes, do tricks on bikes, form a bike club—the possibilities were limitless. Before you discovered the awareness of bike riding, none of this was available. Of course, you also discover how the leg of jeans can get caught in a chain, how traffic creates physical risks, how essential it is to keep the tires and chains maintained… you become aware of a whole new universe of information. You probably also became aware of how knee tissue regenerates but jeans don't. Some catch, that Catch 22!

Similarly, as you unlock your potential and bring it forward, as you become aware of it, everything that goes with the different levels of awareness becomes yours as you traverse them one by one.

Remember:

> **If you weren't equal to it…
> it would not have appeared
> in your awareness.**

# CHAPTER SEVEN

*Working with the
Law of Polarity*

You might be wondering how to look at where you are right now, at your current results—the level of income you don't want, the lifestyle you don't want—without getting caught in a cause-and-effect loop that reinforces those results. Remember, when you perceive a negative result with your physical eyes, that information goes into your conscious mind, which forms an image of what you perceive. As Wallace Wattles says in *The Science of Getting Rich*, "To look upon the appearance of poverty will produce corresponding forms in your own mind."

Then, both consciously and subconsciously, you evaluate that result. You take a neutral fact and add a value judgment to it. Your subconscious mind responds with an emotion: you don't like it. You reinforce this response with a *story*. That story causes you to think certain thoughts and, guided by those thoughts, to take the actions which produce the corresponding result. You see that result with your physical eyes— and the sequence continues. You keep creating the

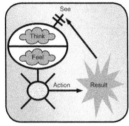

same external reality over and over again. The squiggly lines in the body of the Dr. Fleet's stick person represent the negativity that becomes a habit because of this cycle you're experiencing.

When you find yourself caught in a loop like this, the first thing to do is to *understand it*.

It's not that the result is bad in itself. It's just something *you don't want*.

One of the most important first things to do is to *be grateful for the loop*, because it's letting you know where you are! CRITICAL information, huh!?

Second, realize that being stuck in this kind of loop is simply a matter of not understanding how to move forward. It's not that you can't move; you just don't know how. Or perhaps you're not moving forward because you don't want to make a mistake. That basic motive, wanting to do what's right, is good. However, your fear is preventing you from making the kind of change that will bring results you really *do* want.

In such moments, the Law of Polarity is the universal law to study, because it reveals *why* change is possible as well as *how* to change. This law says: Everything in creation has its opposite. Every up has a down, and every down has an up. There is no inside to a room without an outside. If this side of the page is the front, then the other side is the back.

Not only does everything have an opposite, but that opposite is also *equal.* If the distance from the floor to the table is three feet, then the distance from the table to the floor is three feet also. If it is 750 miles from New York to Chicago, it must be 750 miles from Chicago to New York. It cannot be any other way.

By this same law: every question has an answer. So also, you cannot have an idea without the *way* to carry out that idea being present simultaneously. This is why anything you can think of is possible. If it weren't possible, you couldn't think it. Why? Because all ideas originate in limitless Source, and so do the ways and means to manifest those ideas.

Think for just a second about ideas. They burst into your awareness. They just *show up.* Do you do anything to produce them. Sure! You pay attention and direct your focus. But the ideas… they just *show up*. And they show up in direct proportion to your ability to take the next step toward moving the idea toward reality.

## Connecting a Mental Image with Spiritual Energy

You have the power to choose which images you hold in your mind, which then produce results in your life. How is that? A great spiritual energy coming from

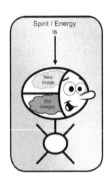

Source flows to and through every person. Picture it as a white, beaming, all-potential light coming right in through the crown of your head and illuminating your entire body.

This figure shows that energy going right into the conscious mind. The light or energy itself is without form. You give form to that energy by what you choose to think, for the Universe has gifted us with the power of choice.

Although spirit is without form, it is not without purpose. What is its purpose? How do you determine that? Start with Universal Rule 1 - More Life to all.

You can see this principle at work all through nature. Everything that goes in grows out. If a seed falls to the ground and is in the right environment, it will grow. The only reason it won't grow is if its environment doesn't support it.

All of nature is for *More Life*. The purpose of all spirit, all energy, that flows to you is *More Life for you*. It will grow whatever you hold in your mind.

You can use that energy to form a negative image and grow that in your life. This is why a drug addict becomes more of a drug addict, an alcoholic becomes more of an alcoholic, a murderer becomes more of a murderer. On the other hand, a person who uses that energy to form a positive image becomes more of what that image is. A person who builds a great business builds a greater business. A person who helps people helps more people.

In *The Science of Getting Rich,* Wallace Wattles refers to this energy or light in many different ways so people of all faiths and beliefs can relate to it. He calls it God, Spirit, Nature, the Universe, Intelligence, Supreme Intelligence, and the thinking substance. Use whatever term for it you feel comfortable with.

He says in one place, "The thinking substance is friendly to you and is more anxious to give you what you want than you are to get it."

If I were you, I would take this quote off the page and put it up on the wall in your office or home or even on your bathroom mirror where you can see it every morning.

Can you conceive that the Universe wants to give you what you want more than you want to receive it? Why would that possibly be? Our ego gets in the way, keeping us from being open to receive what is ours to receive.

## Attuning the Conscious and Subconscious Mind

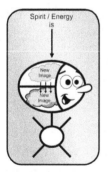

Once you have created an image of what you want in your conscious mind, the next step is to impress that image upon your subconscious mind, as this figure illustrates.

You can do this best by staying emotionally involved with the image *without wavering.* If your emotions about your new idea are unsteady, you risk connecting a negative emotion to it and pushing it away from you.

What does this mean? The image you hold has very little power in itself. Much more important is what you *feel* about what you *think.*

The random thinking that passes through your conscious mind has very little power, until you mix it with emotion. Emotion is the engine that drives your thoughts through time and space. The author and teacher Dr. Raymond Holliwell points out, "... when mixed with emotion, our thoughts travel through space 930,000 times faster than the speed of our voice."[vii]

Emotion is the most powerful energy we know of. When you take a thought and mix it with emotion, you send it flying out across the cosmos. It resonates with like energy, and everything that is in harmony with it starts coming back to you. This is the Law of Vibration and Attraction.

You might be thinking: "That's a stretch, David. I don't know if I believe that."

The reason why people don't believe it is because they haven't *experienced it* consistently and successfully. And they haven't experienced it consistently and successfully because they're making an error without even knowing it.

Here is how the cycle can go if people aren't being intentional and recognizing the power at their disposal:

The person first forms an image on the screen of their mind and she mixes it with the positive emotion of wanting that thing. So far – so good. But the next day she attaches a different emotion to it—usually *doubt* that she will ever receive that thing. There now exist conflicting, emotion-powered orders in the Universe. The Universe was already moving what she wanted toward her, but because she didn't see it forming and heading her way immediately, the next day she repelled it with a negative emotion.

Here's an illustration: The room you're in right now has all kinds of broadcasts—rock and roll, gospel, talk radio, sports, weather, jazz, country, classical, you name it—every kind of radio, satellite, television, brain waves—all running through it. But to perceive any of them you need an attuned receiver. This receiver, this radio, has to be *plugged in*—it needs an energy source. And it has to be *tuned* to a specific frequency to pick up the broadcast you want to hear.

Let's say you turn the radio on and tune it to a frequency that is carrying jazz music, but you don't like jazz. You can't stand it. In fact, it drives you up the wall. You sit in your chair and say, "I really wish I was not listening to jazz. I wish somebody would turn on a classical station. Why won't this station just play classical?"

It can't. It's programmed to produce the result of jazz, and jazz only. If you want to change what you're hearing, you have to imagine what you want, make a decision, and take an action. The action requires change: you are sitting down and now you have to get up. Then you have to adapt to the change: you have to walk over to the radio. And you need the understanding, the skill, to change the radio to a station that is going to bring you classical music.

Here is an important note that may seem too obvious to mention but is critical to any of this taking place: you have to believe there <u>actually is</u> a classical station and a <u>way to find it.</u> Otherwise you won't move from your chair.

In fact *any* time you are sitting in inaction when the only way to alter change is through action it is because you do not *believe* that the action will move you toward your goal. If you did, you would act. Wouldn't you?

The other thing that will stop you is: not *knowing* how the action you are about to take will get you there. There is more than a little merit in the idea that ANY action away from where you are is movement toward where you need to be. Even when the action takes you farther from your goal, the action of moving and checking where you are *showed you* the right direction.

(Remember our first two artillery shots and how much we learned from not hitting the target?) All you have to do is react and change. Why don't we? Because we are often more afraid of *being wrong because we made a choice* than we are of sticking with what we (four letter word alert…) *know.*

We accept the reality of the world of radio because somebody revealed it to us. If you go back far enough in history—and you don't have to go back that far—radio wasn't even a concept. But now we can sit in a room and listen to whatever music we choose. It's a matter of tuning into the right frequency.

Do you realize that everything you want is also on a specific frequency? Your brain is like the tuner for those frequencies. Your emotions, like a transmitter, shoot whatever your brain is tuned to out across time and space to harmonize with the things you want in your life. Like following a GPS signal, when your frequency meets like frequencies those energies are directed together.

## Which Image, Which Emotion?

Where do you get the image that your brain is tuned to? It's your choice. Unless you make that choice *consciously,* however, you may find yourself on autopilot flying to the destinations others have decided for you. I urge you to choose the image that's in your heart. Then get emotionally involved with it.

You might ask, "What emotion do I express?" Start with *gratitude.* What you desire is already here because you already have it on a conscious level as thought, so why not be grateful for it? If you stay in that emotion, you'll continue to bring it toward you.

> *(The practice of gratitude is essential to the manifestation process. As my gift to you, I invite you to receive instant, no-cost access to the recording, transcript and handout of my teaching on "The Practice of Gratitude." Visit* www.davidneagle.com/transform/gratitude *to begin now!)*

If you take that same image and tack a negative emotion to it, you're repelling it with a negative feeling, and you won't get what you want. You'll get its polar opposite.

When your conscious and subconscious are congruous, then by law whatever you are holding in both must manifest in the physical world, as Sticky's next figure shows.

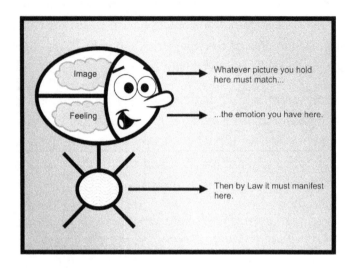

This is the Perpetual Law of Transmutation. In religious terms, it's called prayer.

Most people think prayer is getting down on your knees saying, "God help me." That's just making a noise on your knees. Prayer is spirit moving into form with and through you. It's taking place through you all the time.

## Visualize Your Heart's Desire and Hold It with Your Will

Your subconscious mind cannot tell the difference between a thought in your conscious mind that is registering an actual sensory perception and one that is imagined. It will bring you whatever you impress upon it. If you are in business and want more sales, more effective marketing, better skills, more clients or prospects, all you need to do is build the image and get emotionally involved with that image. The Universe must begin to move those results in your direction. And… you *must have the courage to act on it when it* gets here.

Holding an imagined thought in your conscious mind is what Genevieve Behrend, author of *Your Invisible Power,* calls visualizing. Attaching positive emotions to that thought she speaks of holding the image with your will. In her book Your Invisible Power she writes:

> *The exercise of the visualizing faculty keeps your mind in order, and attracts to you the things you need to make life more enjoyable in an orderly way. If you train yourself in the practice of deliberately picturing your desire and carefully examining your picture, you will soon find that your thoughts and desires proceed in a more orderly procession than ever before. Having reached a state of ordered mentality, you are no longer in a state of mental hurry. Hurry is Fear, and consequently destructive.*

*In other words, when your understanding grasps the power to visualize your heart's desire and hold it with your will, it attracts to you all things requisite to the fulfillment of that picture by the harmonious vibrations of the law of attraction. You realize that since Order is Heaven's first law, and visualization places things in their natural order, then it must be a heavenly thing to visualize.*

*Everyone visualizes, whether they know it or not. Visualization is the great secret of success.*

That passage is beautiful and filled with so much truth, especially the second paragraph. She says: *in other words, when your understanding grasps the power to visualize…. it attracts to you all things requisite to the fulfillment of that picture…"* Understanding happens when we start to *see something differently.* For instance, when we start to see the potential in a teaching, we begin to understand it at a different level.

What does your understanding begin to visualize? *Your heart's desire.* Once you know what your heart's desire is, your understanding is able to grasp the power to visualize it.

*Visualize your heart's desire and hold it with your will.* Will is a higher faculty; one of the spiritual faculties gifted to human beings. No other form of life on the planet that we are aware of has these gifts.

I was raised with the idea that will is something people use to project their authority over someone else. It has nothing do with that. Will is simply a mental muscle. It's the ability to focus on one thing, to hold an idea in your consciousness without interference from any other ideas. It's the same thing as attaching a positive emotion to the image you're visualizing. The positive emotion keeps you engaged. You can develop that skill.

So what is she saying here? *When your understanding grasps the power to visualize your heart's desire and hold it with your will...* In other words, when you become single-minded: You know your heart's desire, you know who you are, where you're going, and what you are going to accomplish.

What happens then? *It attracts to you all things requisite to the fulfillment of that picture by the harmonious vibrations of the law of attraction.* She doesn't say it brings you the thing itself. She says it brings you *everything you need for the manifestation* of that thing.

People visualize receiving money and expect the money to arrive on their front doorstep. That would be nice, but it doesn't work that way. Rather, what comes is opportunities. You have to take the opportunity and work it. You have to actually *do* something.

Behrend writes further: *You realize that since order is heaven's first law and visualization places things in their natural order, then it must be a heavenly thing to visualize.*

We all visualize. The key is to train ourselves to visualize what we want for ourselves, and to eject from our minds the old stories that no longer serve our highest good.

> **If we commit to focusing solely on what we want, the opportunities that will lead to its manifestation will come into our awareness immediately.**

And the really great news is: That's the Law.

# Chapter Eight

## *Embracing Opportunity*

People often assume that major change requires an extended period of time to take place, but this is not necessarily so. One reason it often does take a long time is the major change exists in the mind alongside the prior state with all of the pressures and images to return to that state. That conflict can rage on for lifetimes. So there is a lot of evidence that major change can take a long time. But the time it takes is not a function of the energies needed to affect the change. It is a function of the energies needed to focus on and *accept* the change. The time delay is a product of *resistance* and competing imagery.

Once you have embraced an opportunity, it does not have to take long to see real change. The amount of time is related to a person's level of awareness, which grows continuously with the dedicated application of these teachings. Napoleon Hill studied five hundred of the world's most successful people over a twenty-year period. Some of them had gone through many lean years, and then suddenly, as if a light switch was flipped, everything began to change. He writes:

> *When riches begin to come, they come so quickly, in such great abundance, that one wonders where they have been hiding during all those lean years.*
>
> *This is an astounding statement, all the more so when we take into consideration the popular belief that riches come only to those who work hard and long. When you begin to think and grow rich, you will observe that riches begin with a state of mind, with definiteness of purpose, with little or no hard work.*

Hill's book, *Think and Grow Rich,* contains so much wisdom. I suggest you make it a daily study for the rest of your life. I began reading the book years ago and still study it constantly.

What Hill describes happened in my case. I started off at $20,000 a year and tripled my income in eleven months. Then it kept going—to $20,000 a month,

$50,000 a month, then $60,000 a month. I became fascinated, and not only with what had happened for me. I began to meet other people who had similar experiences. Once they made the decision to change, they began manifesting massive transformation in their lives, as though heaven's gates had opened up for them.

Some of them didn't know what they were doing to make it happen. They had never studied any success literature. In fact, when my life first began to change, I hadn't either. We were what are called unconscious competents. We were *doing the right things* without realizing it and still getting great results. That is a very important point. We were doing the right things. This was not a mysterious business formulae, this was a point of view, and belief. The success was present because we were practicing success behaviors and the millions of resources within manifested as millions of literal *dollars* in our reality.

I think you can see, though, that this kind of success is tenuous, vulnerable and extremely conditional. If an unconscious competent's situation changes drastically or *if fear overtakes them,* they can lose that ability. It will vanish around them and they won't know why. Worse, they won't know how to reignite the "mojo" that had things working to begin with.

We see this all the time in suddenly successful people. They are unconsciously doing the right thing and get the results needed. Then they decide it is *them. They* are the reason... their looks, their intellect, their business genius. Their ego takes over and instead of the right things they were doing they decide they have the Midas touch. An unexpected outcome will throw them. Instead of looking humbly at what mental adjustment must be made, they might take personal offense that the universe could treat them this way. They dig in and "stick to their guns" – the guns that produced the undesired outcome – and get more of the same. Until they wake up and get out from behind their egos that spiral will continue downward.

The unspeakable irony here is that it was their doing. They were doing it right. They didn't know what the right thing they were doing *was!!* Their unconscious competency drove them from the very behaviors that produced the desirable outcomes.

On the other hand, someone who understands how to work with the universal laws can continue to create success even when the situation shifts. Understanding that the results produced in her reality are the product of The Law at work will keep her from the ego-trip of a tantrum and spark in her a new and exciting quest for what is going on here. "What is this outcome – this outcome that I have produced – trying to teach me?" It will be through that gratitude and focus that she will see the misalignment of intentions that resulted in the less than desired outcome. Then she can change that. A mid-course correction without guilt and drama.

We want to understand not only how to manifest change under any circumstances but also what makes it happen fast. To do this, let's first examine what slows down the process of change or stops it. Once we are aware of what doesn't work, we can identify what does.

## The Universe Knows What You Need

When people are first learning to set goals and move toward their heart's desire, they tend to revert to old ways... to their *habitual* behavior and choice patterns. They start to decide, even if only subconsciously, what opportunity they need next, what step they next need to take. A word of caution: *This* will keep you stuck.

The Universe *knows* what you need next better than you do. It may even keep sending you that opportunity. The Universe is saying, "*This* is what you need next." But you don't recognize it because you think you need something else.

A great example of this is the story of the deeply religious and constantly faithful Southern gentleman who heard a flood was coming.

*In spite of flood warnings, the old gentleman faithfully declared that "His Lord" would save him. As the clouds gathered and the weather worsened his neighbors came to help him pack some things and leave. "NO. I have faith that my LORD will save me," he insisted. And they left.*

*Hours later as the deluges came a sheriff's truck stopped to offer assistance. "NO. My LORD will save me," he insisted. So they left.*

*After the rains the river rose and he found himself on his roof with water rising. A boat came by to take him to safety. "NO. I have faith that my LORD will save me," he insisted. So they left.*

*Ultimately the waters rose to the point he was treading water and a Coast Guard helicopter swooped down to pluck him from certain death. "NO. I have faith that my LORD will save me," he insisted. And he went under. And he drowned.*

*A few moments in eternity later he found himself before St. Peter, wet and mad. He railed at St. Peter that his God had let him down. St. Peter was taken aback and quickly began to check the records. The man started in with his tantrum again.*

*"I have always been nothing but faithful, aaaaalways believed, DIED believing that my Lord would save me! And he did NOTHING."*

*Looking up from the record, St. Peter said, "Nothing? Really??? The record says here we sent three neighbors, a sheriff, a boat, and a Coast Guard helicopter."*

I love that story. Here is a guy whose "millions within" were millions of ways to take the evidence before him and deny it. I can recognize that in him because I've seen it in me!

Tony Robbins studied all the great teachers and from them he determined that the function of the ego was to keep a person 1) alive, and 2) right.[x] Not necessarily in that order. In fact, sadly, people too often make the choice to stay in their "rightness" at the cost of their lives and the lives of others. We call this *terrorism* for a reason. It is about as far from "More Life" as you can get. By that measure alone, we should release the need to be right *immediately.*

I experienced this myself but not quite to that extent. The opportunity that I embraced to triple that original $20,000 had been in my presence twice a week for two years. TWO YEARS. That is close to 700 sunrises that had shined their light on the very thing I was seeking, right there in my presence. But because I was looking for something else—and because I was so frustrated, so negative, so stubborn, and had such a poor attitude—I literally did not see it. And like our drowning man of faith, I was a bit ticked off about it a lot of the time.

A good friend of mine used to say, "The first place you go blind is in the eye." There's a word used in psychological circles for that blind spot in the mind: "scotoma." Have you ever observed one person say something to another and the listener understand something completely different from what the first person said? That's the listener's scotoma at work.

One hilarious example of how this works is Abbott and Costello's "Who's on First" routine. As a member of the audience we can understand both parties' points of view and it is a slap-your-knee riot… for us. For the characters in the miscommunication, it is frustrating and fear producing. If you are one of the three people on the planet unfamiliar with this work of comedic genius, search the internet for Abbott and Costello's "Whose on First." You can thank me later.

Just like Lou Costello, our expectations can leave us blind (in his case, *deaf*) to the opportunities around us.

Most people would say, "Show me an opportunity for the kind of rapid success you had, David. I will see it. Any idiot could see it." I have news for you. The opportunity for you to bring in money like that is already around you, *but you're not aware of it—and you won't be aware of it* **until you start to change your perception.**

STOP.

Pay attention to how you are feeling about that statement. Does that excite you and make you eager to make the change that you do not yet see or understand? Or, are you feeling frustration, anger, and tension because you just can't see it and don't want to be responsible for the state your life is in presently? Don't judge it... notice it.

Be *grateful* for that information. It is the key to your change! You are standing at the door of opportunity right now as you read these words. *This very second!!* If you, 1) *are aware* that this has a negative emotional charge for you, and 2) the source of that negative perspective is outside of your conscious choice - then you can now step in and *change that!* You can decide – right here and now – that the opportunity you need has been around you for weeks – months – maybe all your life. And *now* you have a chance to uncover it and put it into action.

Have you ever lost the keys to the car... in the house? You can't see them. You absolutely, without a single shadow of doubt are *certain* that those danged keys are *right here* somewhere... but you can't see them. Ever had that happen? This awareness needs to be like that. You need to have that level of absolute, total certainty that what you need is already right there around you. You aren't going to find those keys by raging around looking for them. Most likely you need to relax, breathe (a few times), and then look with new eyes. Let them reveal themselves to you. If you insist... they may continue to hide.

Napoleon Hill called this "the sly disguise of opportunity:"

> *When opportunity came, it appeared in a different form and from a different direction than he had expected. That is one of the tricks of opportunity. It has a sly habit of slipping in*

*by the back door, and often it comes disguised in the form of misfortune, or temporary defeat. Perhaps this is why so many people fail to recognize opportunity.*

The first time I read that, I jumped right out of my chair. I hadn't seen the opportunity *right in front of me* because it looked like misfortune, like something I didn't want. And then, for a second, I thought, "It can't be that easy." But, I got over that. It was *precisely* that easy. C'mon... the keys are *in the house!*

People are so convinced that success can only come a *certain* way. They don't recognize that the neighbors, the sheriff, the boat, and the helicopter are for *them!!* So they should be turning their attention there... and get busy climbing on board!

## Is This Opportunity Right For Me?

Once you do recognize an opportunity that has come into your life, how do you determine whether or not it truly is the next step to take? After all, you have more than just the consciously driven motives in your spirit. Perhaps this opportunity has been called up by one of your lesser desires or old programming or your unconscious. How do you *discern* the true value and applicability of the opportunity before you? Particularly since the unconscious has insidious ways of calling upon every ounce of your history to find attractive distractions: distractions that will look promising, cloud your judgment and thinking, and keep you right where you are with movement that looks for all the world to be goal-driven.

What, then, is the test for *authenticity to purpose?*

The best way is by asking these four questions:

1. Is this opportunity something my heart wants to be, do, or have?

2. Is being, doing, or having this going to take me closer to my goal?

3. Is being, doing, or having this in harmony with the nature of the Universe, which is: More Life?

4. Is being, doing, or having this going to honor and not violate the rights of others? (The right we are mainly concerned with here is other people's choice. We don't want to take away another person's freedom to choose.)

None of these questions says anything about having enough money, having enough time, or whether other people are backing you up—whether your spouse approves, or who is going to watch the kids. These are the wrong issues to drag in when opportunities come into your life. These old excuses are the stories you have created about why you can't change. Put them aside.

Also, these questions must be answered in order. If you don't get a "Yes" to the first… you are done. This is not the opportunity for you.

If you do get a yes to "Want" you must then get a yes to "movement toward the goal." If not… this is not the opportunity for you.

You need a solid "Yes" to the "More Life" question and this one can get tricky. I have a very dear friend who was in a marriage that she could see was not working for her. It was not ugly or abusive or horrible, but her husband could not and would not accept the growth and change she was going through. She got stuck on question three because to end that marriage and move into the path she saw before her seemed to be more life for *her*, but not for *him*. It seemed selfish.

After much soul searching and self-examination it occurred to her that to stay would mean she was living a lie, and the life he was living would be a lie as well. For her to pursue her true self would force him out of the comfort zone he had crawled into. He wouldn't like it and would fight it. But to stay would to mean *less* life for her most certainly. They did get a divorce and he did have a hard time of it. And she did feel some guilt. But she also saw that he had opportunities of his own to pursue, to grow… and that if he did *not*… then that was his choice. She came to believe that her decision created the opportunity for more life for both of them, but whether he took advantage of that or not was not her business. She determined, after very careful examination, that she had a "Yes" to question three. Her decision created more life for all, and less for none.

Then you need a clean "No" on the last question. Nothing good ever came from a benefit to one that cost another the right to choose. You feel the rightness of that inside, don't you? Even in the example of the divorce above, the ex-husband had and continues to have freedom to choose how he will live his life.

## Letting Go to Move Forward

When you are presented with an opportunity and it is in harmony with those four questions, you need to *act on it.* This is another point where people stop— because of what the opportunity requires of them.

You see, there is another law:

> **When you want something of a higher nature in your life, you have to give up something of a lower nature.**

This is the true definition of "sacrifice."

Opportunities that can move you to a new level of awareness and all that it offers usually require sacrifice of some kind. The sacrifice might be in the form of money, time, study, work, risk, or other changes to your current lifestyle.

If you say, "I fully accept whatever sacrifice I have to make in order to make this change," then it is not difficult at all. Difficulty lies only in resisting the change. It is resistance that brings about a long delay in manifesting your heart's desire.

I asked one entrepreneur at the close of a brief conversation at another speaker's seminar: "What is your next step?"

He said, "It's to purchase a program that costs $1,400."

I said, "Great. Get the program and get going."

"I don't have the money."

"Do you mean to tell me that you know this program is what's going to turn your business around and you don't have the money? What are you waiting for? If you need it, the money for it has to be there.

"But I don't have the money in my account."

"You're not looking closely enough, because the opportunity for you to get the money is right in front of you."

Roadblocks are not God's denials; they are the results of what you think about his gifts. (Hello! Neighbors, sheriffs, boats, helicopters!) People let doubt and fear grip their mind and keep them in their misery. But you can't move forward – and also stay where you are.

## Breaking through the Fear

To speed up the process of change there is one simple but serious decision you must make: You must decide to accept with pleasure the change that is required. No kidding.

Do it with joy even if you are scared at first. After doing this a few times, you will discover that change is wonderful. You will actually look forward to it.

One of the enormously powerful and totally unsung benefits of embracing change and walking into the unknown is that it demystifies the unknown. The only power the unknown has is your ability to imagine disaster. If you stepped in without fear but *with* complete awareness and alertness to the situations and circumstances around you, the likelihood is you could handle whatever new stuff pops up with only minor delays and detours. Even the major ones, though, are in your favor.

If, on your journey, you end up in a two-month (or two-year) side trip battling old fears that you have categorized as "facts of life" you will come to a brand new place in your life. It will be a place from which you will have unlimited options instead of the one or two roads that you allowed yourself when dealing with these old fears and limiting beliefs before.

Until you see these issues as mere vectors of force and make allowances for how they affect the world around them they will be "dark mysteries of the inner sanctum." But once you see them, cope with them, allow for them – *deal* with them – they are just variables to be aware of and possibly even *use* to your advantage in other situations.

Do you see how much *power* that gives you? To be able to step into the unknown and not be fearful? To know that you are equal to whatever may greet you and that even if it isn't what you might desire or expect it is *precisely* the issue you must deal with to get where you want to go??? How great a promise is THAT?

I understand how challenging this is. People used to tell me, too, when an opportunity came my way and I didn't have the money to embrace it, that I didn't want it badly enough; that if I really wanted it, I would find a way. I would get so upset: "That's just not true. You have no idea how badly I want this."

Then one day a friend put it this way: "David, you have kids, right? Let's say that a kidnapper took one of your kids and was threatening to kill that child unless you came up with a certain amount of money within a week. Would you come up with the money?"

"Absolutely."

"What just changed? A minute ago you said you didn't have the money, and now you are confident that you could come up with it." Then he added: "You would beg, borrow, or steal to get the money to save your children, but you won't do the same to save yourself."

That got me thinking. "Oh my God, I really *don't* want it badly enough. I'm coming up against my fear. I'm coming right to the edge of my comfort zone and then stepping right back to where I was."

I have seen people who have studied this material for years do the same thing. They won't break through that uncomfortable place. What is stopping them from reaching out for what is already theirs? They're afraid of what somebody else is going to think (their spouse, for instance); they're afraid they're not yet ready; they're afraid their existing clients won't like the new direction their business is taking.

One trick to breaking through fears is to simply take action. My mentor's mentor, Leland Val Vanderwal, said, "Doing at once what must be done will ensure the possibility of success."

The moment you become aware of what you have to do next, do it. Don't think about it. Ask yourself those four questions, and then make the decision – and *act*.

The word "de-cision" means to cut off any other possibility. If you leave yourself another possibility, you leave yourself a story. You leave yourself an out. You may be thinking, "Isn't that what I'm supposed to do— have a plan B?" No. Napoleon Hill wrote that we have to burn the ships. We have to sever the possibility of retreating from what we are supposed to do.

This may sound difficult. It isn't. I do this every day and don't find it difficult. Not now. But I used to find it *tremendously* difficult. Why? Because I was battling the unseen demons I described a few pages back.

It is the fears built up in your mind that are difficult. The old folk wisdom says the word "fear" is an acronym for "false evidence appearing real." When you remain stuck due to fear, you are letting imagined ghosts scare you into stopping short of doing what you are supposed to do.

When you break through fear often enough, you come to understand that the fear isn't real. As you grow comfortable with fear you begin to master it. Then the change that you really want begins to happen quickly – and without "effort."

# CHAPTER NINE

## Viewing Money As a Tool

Money comes up often in the discussion of success because money is often both a tool to achieving success and a scoreboard of having achieved it. So I want to look at *money* and the related topic of *prosperity* in some detail.

What is money? Like everything else in our material world, money is nothing but energy that has manifested into physical form through the realization of an idea.

In days past, when people wanted to acquire services and products, they traded things of value, such as pigs, chickens, or beads.

Before we go any further, look at those things of "value" and see that the value lies in the represented energy of those things. Whether for a meal, breeding stock, a pet (the pig maybe, but chickens?), or a symbol of trade – they *all* are *energy* stored as a physical *thing.*

> **The big idea here is that everything is energy –stored in another form.**

This is a critical concept; energy gets stored in physical form. (Hey! This will be on the test and counts for about 90% of your grade, so pay attention here.)

And *money* is one of those forms that is most readily exchanged for most of the other forms. Of itself, the only value money holds is for the heat and energy it would release being burned.

As civilization developed, trading became more and more difficult. You might have pigs to barter, but if the person whose goods or services you wanted didn't need any pigs, you had a problem. So the idea of a monetary symbol – money – was conceived.

Initially, the abstract nature of the concept was hard to believe in or agree to. Coin, minted in precious metals that were equal in value to the thing traded was easier to accept. I give you a five-dollar chicken and I will feel okay about five dollars worth (weight) of gold or copper or silver. So, a five dollar gold piece was, itself, worth five dollars. Sometimes, when the sum was large enough that transporting it would be difficult or dangerous, a *Note* would be written; a contract, signed by a person of good reputation, which stated the note itself was exchangeable for a certain amount of gold or goods. Here we step into the abstraction of paper money... exchanging something of low intrinsic value that represents *HIGH* intrinsic value.

That "note" idea was the birth of currency. The idea of a currency that was a "note" signed by a government or state was introduced and paper money, the components of which are worth far less than the face value printed on it, became popular. These paper documents were not worth five dollars themselves, but were "notes"; promises, contracts-to-deliver the worth of the face value... on demand.

But currency is not money. Currency is paper. Money is an *idea.* The idea of money is nothing more than the idea of transferable energy. Remember... 90% on the quiz. (No, not my quiz, silly. Life's.)

What has caused such corruption around the idea of money? In a broad sense, the abuse of power. We should *love people* and *use money.* The concept of money becomes corrupt when people begin to *love money* and *use people.*

Many throughout history have bought into that view. In fact, the entire fear community would have you believe it is a principle of truth; that money, control, power – all of these are related. Search your own internal beliefs about money to see if this rings true in your learnings. It is not true. The truth is that we can use money as a means to better our lives without taking on that view.

## Money Misconceptions

It is said: "There is nothing as powerful as a concept and nothing more dangerous than a misconception." Misconceptions about money are usually among the beliefs we absorb unconsciously from our parents or society, and they can keep us in or near poverty all our days... voluntarily.

One such misconception concerns the relationship between money and happiness. Some people believe that if they have money they will be happy. Others say money will never make you happy. Both ideas are absurd because money was never meant to make you happy. Money is a tool to help make you comfortable by simplifying the exchanges of energy.

Another misconception almost everyone has bought into is that money has value. Let's take a second to unpack that notion.

Though gold has found a number of very valuable applications in the micro-technology computer age, initially its values were: 1) it was pretty, and 2) it was scarce. That's it. It couldn't really DO much for you initially except make some piece of jewelry you wore cause you to look physically more attractive than someone who didn't have gold jewelry. And if they *did* have jewelry, your recourse was to have *more* or bigger and gaudier jewelry than they had. Now there is real value for you. Total imagined worth! The emperor's new clothes. Shiny objects!

Kingdoms were exchanged for this *perception* of value. So, at the root of it, even the precious metal's actual "worth" is merely a matter of scarcity and perception. It is argued that if a deep-sea diver discovered Atlantis and hidden within it a billion cubic meters of gold stashed away – the price of gold would plummet *instantly.* Entire global economies would collapse. Not because its value changed... but because its *scarcity* did.

So, if even *gold* has no true value... what does? Is there anything that truly has value and that will impact the experience of your life?

Absolutely there is. And you already have as much of it as everyone else does each day. The fact is *time* is the only real thing of value, since it's the one truly limited resource. Most people, if they think for even a few seconds, will tell you that what they value most is their time on this planet and how they spend it. On a person's dying day, how much money wouldn't they be willing to spend for a little more time with the people they love?

I don't think you can put a monetary value on time. Yet most people spend their days trading their magnificent lives for money; time for dollars. Ironically, even sadly, the energy they have left (and no small amount of their money) is then spent trying not to lose that money. What a vicious cycle.

Do you really believe this is what we were supposed to be doing? Every second, minute, hour, day, and year you trade for money is time you never get back!

Another common misconception, one that people often carry deep down inside, is that it's *wrong* to have money. If you doubt this, sit down with your closest family and friends and announce that you are going to become fantastically wealthy. Then notice how you feel inside. That will tell you what you believe about money. Then ask those people what they think about your idea. That will give you some insight as to who is influencing your choices. Be careful with this experiment if you are not prepared to know what people truly think. There is no going back.

What other misconceptions about money are you carrying? Be brutally honest with yourself. What did you hear about money as you were growing up? What comments were made about successful people, about success itself?

Most of the ideas we were taught regarding money actually repel us from it. Then we go through life trying to get something that deep down inside we are rejecting. This mixed message produces nothing but mixed results.

## From Lower to Higher Potential Perpetuates Lack

All of these misconceptions about money are based on the same measurement as the value of gold: an assumption of limitation – scarcity. We have been conditioned to orient ourselves according to the world around us, to what we can see *with our eyes*. The physical world is made up of finite things. A limited, *finite* number of things. When that is your orientation you see *need*, which causes you presume *limitation* and *lack*. All you see are problems. I call this working from a lower to a higher potential.

Most people have been programmed subconsciously this way. They grow up hearing: "We don't have enough."

"That's too expensive; we can't afford it." "That's a nice opportunity and if we just had the money, we could do it."

That thinking gives form to the spiritual energy that is flowing to and through all of us. That energy's purpose is to grow whatever idea you give it. What happens then? The idea of limitation is reinforced.

Since 2006 or so there has been a perception that the world is broke. Not just Europe, not just Greece, not just the USA... everyone. Global economies are collapsing – according to the headlines. Now, the fact is there are still just as many houses (more!) as there were in 2005, as many cars (more), as many farms, etc. What "IS" has not changed that much (except to increase according to the laws of More Life). But there is an almost universal agreement that things are bad and getting worse. And because it is a universally held belief, it is manifesting just as the rules say it should.

Here again, widely held beliefs produce widely visible results to match those beliefs. Early in Jesus' ministry he went to his hometown. They didn't think of him as "the Messiah" there, they though of him as "Joe's oldest. The carpenter's kid." Jesus went to the temple and told the town that the prophesies of a promised Messiah had been fulfilled. He was it. This did NOT fit with their image of "the carpenter's kid." They tried to kill him but he ducked out. In fact, he "was able to do nothing, for their lack of belief." When even the Son of God can get stymied by widely held lack of faith, is it any wonder you and I and our world can get held hostage by it? He very wisely moved on to places that would hear what he had to say. Good example for us! Look at what we're up against, though.

People are taught early on to stop fantasizing, to deal with the reality of limitation, and to base their decisions on what others have told them is the truth. They want to succeed; yet they're programmed to merely survive.

According to Webster's dictionary, "survive" means "to remain alive or in existence." That's no way to live. You're not designed to live that way. You are born with the potential to lead a magnificent life.

Because they believe that there is "never enough," survivors are always looking for opportunities to *get*. "I want to *get* the deal. I want to *get* the bargain. I need to *get* a better job." Underneath their desire to get, they're trying to fill a perceived need for love, security, and self-esteem.

Everything in the survivor's world confirms what they believe: The are not *enough*, and there isn't *enough*. And guess what? They can prove it. They'll tell you: "Look at my checkbook. Look at my job, my spouse, my income.

Look at my bills, my debt." When they hear other people talking about their successes, they say, "They're boasting. I don't want to listen to that nonsense." In Nazareth, they ran Jesus out of town. Then they talk about their own problems, or other people's problems. When they tire of that, they turn on the television and listen to the dramas being broadcast there. After all, "Global financial collapse" is a much more dramatic headline than, "Happy days are here if you want to make them that way."

They spend thirty, fifty, seventy years stuck in a survivor's lifestyle. Yet, even with global agreement that the world is ending, even with disaster and collapse at every turn, throughout those years – something is stirring inside their soul saying that life should be different. There is a spark within them that is certain this picture is all wrong. Our spiritual nature never stops trying to lead us toward our highest good, our limitless potential, and the truth that *nothing* is limited.

The Hubble telescope has allowed scientists and physicists to look backward through time to the very birth of the universe. I won't run you through the math and, to tell the truth, I don't get it myself, but the conclusion resonates perfectly with my own spirit. These physicists say that to understand the Big Bang and the creation of *everything* that took place in a million,

million, million, millionth of a second – to get a well-trained scientific mind around that idea – you have to believe that before that moment there was – *nothing*. You have to come to believe that everything… all of the matter in the universe that came into being in that tiny moment… was pure, immeasurable, unperceivable *energy* in the moment before it. This science postulates that in that infinitesimally small instant of time, unimaginable quantities of energy condensed into matter… and *became*… and started moving outward.

Talk about millions within!

## From Higher to Lower Potential Is *Art*

When I was a kid, one of the questions that used to run through my mind was: "Why the heck are so many people miserable if there is a loving God?" I learned the reason later on: they are not taught where to look.

It has been said many times over that God gives us the resources to accomplish what we are put on earth to do. The mistake is to think those resources are outside of ourselves. Think about how different our experience would be *if we believed* that God had *already given* us the resources to accomplish what we are put on earth to do!

Well… that is how it truly is. Change the tense of the verb and the entire reality shifts. God, Allah, the

Universe, SOURCE – will not "give" us what we need… She/He/It already "gave" us what we need. We have it. It exists. It is here.

Like the air that we breathe, it is around us and ready for use every second of the day. But unlike the air – which is outside of us – it is within. It is not in the DNA or the cellular structure, it is in the force that gives those elements life. It is in the power to have an idea and to sustain that idea with focus and energy until it becomes perceivable in the physical realm.

Your amazing, wonderful physical body exchanges the elemental contents of every molecule within it constantly. The very component atoms are changed out through the process of living. It is calculated that every atom in your body is changed out about every 7 years. Once your body dies, that stops. But while you are alive everything about you is in a constant state of change. You have water molecules in you at this moment that were in the body of Christ. And Hitler. And very likely, Bobby Joe from Junior High. You are not your body. You are a spirit occupying and enlivening a body; a spirit of equal power to every spirit that has enlivened every body since the beginning.

Just as your body is refreshed with ingestion, digestion, waste removal and so on, your spirit, likewise, is refreshed by truth. Awareness and truth build up the connection between your spirit and your conscious identity. Falseness separates them. Or worse, it directs the power of that spirit to the destruction of the identity and the body. We know this as dis-ease. It is not a conscious choice. But it is a choice. Our mission is to become conscious enough to be responsible for those choices and for the outcomes of our lives.

I cannot tell you how many times people have said to me, "If God wants me to do this, he will provide the way." In fact, God has already provided the way. (Hello! Four neighbors, a sheriff, a boat and a helicopter!) He gave you the resources built right into who you are as a spiritual being.

When you understand that your resources come from an unlimited universal supply and that you have been gifted with the ability to transform your own belief system and to mine those resources, your world opens up to *unlimited* possibilities. That is not hyperbole. There are no limits to spirit connected to universal supply. None. You begin working from a higher to a lower potential.

This reversal is more than a play on words. People often ask me, "What did you do differently when you discovered it was easier to earn large sums of money than small sums of money?" This is what I did. I learned to work from higher to lower potential.

How do you begin? Start by acknowledging that you live in an infinite Universe where all possibilities exist. That may sound like a grandiose idea, but it's the truth. Everything ever formed by human hands was an idea in somebody's mind first. Where did the idea come from? It came from the Universe, the repository of all possibilities.

Take the cell phone as an example. A century ago, if you had announced that someday people would talk on some instrument to someone on the other side of the world and see the person's picture simultaneously, they would have sent the boys in the white coats to come get you. As recently as the *Star Trek* television series in the 1960s, the flip phone was only science fiction. Where did the idea for a cell phone start? It started in someone's imagination. Though it may have developed in the details, the *idea* itself exploded into the mind of the receiver and the magic is – the receiver was on and paying attention! That person had to believe in the idea and get emotionally involved in it for it to become a physical reality. But the *idea* came from spirit.

How many ideas have you had in your lifetime? How many times has the universe tapped you on the shoulder and asked you to come out and play? Of the ones of which you are aware, there are probably tens of thousands that slipped by unheard in the chaos of surviving the day and the false fears that surround you. Don't feel bad. It isn't like there's a limited supply. More are coming. THIS is one. All you have to do is start participating in a different way.

When you work from higher to lower potential, you take a thought inspired by the desire in your heart and infuse it with formless spiritual energy, which carries the potential for growth and creativity. From that energy and thought you form a new idea. As you get emotionally involved with that idea, you take the actions that move it into form.

This is creativity, and it is evident in any form of art. The artist gets enormous satisfaction from the creation process, and humanity benefits from the product. It's a win-win. Similarly, when you create your life as an expression of the desire in your heart, your life becomes a work of art. Your life is a success, it benefits both yourself and everyone you meet. And you become a successful person.

A successful person is a thriver. Look up "thrive" in the dictionary. It means, "to grow luxuriantly." Now that sounds like living!

Thrivers know that love, security, and self-esteem are available to them on the inside so they don't have to go out and get them. Instead, they go out and *give* them. It's always a pleasure to be around these people because they give their best to everyone in service each day. They give love. They gladly offer recognition to others. They're able to freely express themselves. They know what they want and where they're going. They are filled with purpose that springs forth from the true desire in their heart.

When you are a thriver, you see the opportunities that the Universe sends you as opportunities to give, not to get. Yet as the saying goes, "you reap what you sow." You give to your world and are repaid by the Universe.

## Let the Heart Lead and Prosperity Will Follow

The thriver's mindset is known as prosperity consciousness—an unfaltering belief in abundance and in your ability to create exactly what you need when you need it. When you develop prosperity consciousness, you can't keep money away. It keeps coming in because it has real purpose—it is supporting the expression of your heart's desire. The desire comes first and the money follows.

Let yourself dream about what you really want. Design your life exactly as you dream it. Then make the decision to receive the funds that will allow you to live that life.

What happens next will amaze you. The Universe will send you the opportunities to manifest the money. You have to be on the lookout for them. And when they arrive, they will always be a step up. They'll require that you step up and out in faith to receive what you've asked for. But you'll be inspired to take that step of faith because you have a plan, and you know you're on the way to creating what you truly desire. This is making art with your life.

## CHAPTER TEN

*Finding Your*
*Proper Environment*

Take any seed, put it on the palm of your hand, and ask yourself, "What is it that I'm holding?" You're holding the potential for something else.

If you're holding the seed of a tree, it has the potential for another tree in it. But you are also holding much more than that. The potential for an entire forest lies inside the seed.

If you plant that seed in the proper environment, nurture it, water it, and give it the necessary nutrients, that seed is going to live out its potential. And it doesn't have to work to do it. It does it naturally, effortlessly. It does what it's designed to do. All along the way, it does what is "next." That process creates another tree, which creates another tree, which creates another tree, and before you know it, you have an entire forest.

Every person has a desire in their heart. That desire arrived at this time, in this place, with the person. It isn't an interest that developed over time as the individual matured and became aware. Rather, the desire was there all the time. It is the product of that individual's purpose. The desire is not the purpose. The desire is the *hunger* for the components necessary to make manifest the purpose.

This is one of the reasons that the most important question to answer in "the four questions" is the first one: Is this something I truly want to do, be, or have? The most important question you can answer at any junction of life is, "What do I want?"

When you ask yourself that question, pay close and careful attention to what comes up. It will evolve and grow over time. As you climb the steps of awareness the facets of the diamond of what you want will become more and more clear.

The purpose for which this individual has become manifest in this reality resonates with the billions of variations of resources that will be needed to support the development of that purpose in this reality. That resonance is the desire recognizing a component necessary to fulfill purpose.

That desire is a seed. The desire in your heart holds all the potential for your life locked up right inside.

Take a seed... a kernel of corn... in your hand. It looks like a chubby, flat-sided balloon with a white crusty tip. That tip is the spirit of that kernel. The big yellow balloon contains the nutrients needed for it to become the root, the stem, the blade, the stalk, the ear, the tassel... the field... the tens of millions of fields that will come. Even CORN comes with millions within.

If we place that seed of your desire, surrounded by the kernel of promised *source* – all the resources it will ever need – in the correct environment and it's nurtured, loved, and grows, it can produce unbelievable things in your life. And not just in your life but in the lives of everybody you come in contact with throughout your lifetime.

The seed in your heart can even unlock the seeds that are in all of those people. Why is that? When you become a living expression of your own potential, other people who are looking to access their potential cannot help but notice you. You pass on the inspiration just by being what you are. You don't have to think about it. It just happens.

## Every Seed Needs a Nurturing Environment

For a seed to grow, however, it needs a proper, nurturing environment. Imagine for a moment that you are holding a long-stemmed rose, fully bloomed and open, in your right hand, and in your left hand you are holding a stem from the same rosebush that has only a bud on it. That bud has the same potential as the blossomed flower, but it has not yet had the chance to open. If it is not put into water soon, it never will. Why? Because, it is not in an environment that can nurture it.

We humans are much the same. If we are not in a nurturing environment—perhaps we consciously chose to leave a nurturing environment or we were never raised in one to begin with—we cannot express our full potential. It's not that the potential isn't there. It's absolutely there. But for you to grow and blossom into your full magnificence, being and receiving everything you could possibly desire, you must put yourself in the right environment.

Each of us carries a unique heart's desire that the world needs to see expressed. Myles Munroe says in *Releasing Your Potential,* "The fact that you were born is evidence that God knew earth needed the potential that you're pregnant with. It is therefore imperative that you refuse to leave this planet without giving birth to those dreams, ideas, visions and inventions that you carry in the womb of your faith right now."*xii* Think about that. What you have locked up inside of you is needed in the world.

But if you take the seed of a tree and crush it, not only do you kill the seed, you kill a whole forest. What happens when we do not put an individual in the right environment where he or she can blossom? The person's ability to step into their fullest potential is hindered. Maybe the person had the potential to be a great poet or musician, or a wonderful architect, or to write beautiful literature. Perhaps that person could have been the one to find a cure for cancer or AIDS. Instead, he or she goes through life in lack and limitation, and the world misses the benefits that person could have brought.

## Choosing What Supports Your Growth

If you want to grow and create a life of success, pay attention to your current environment. Who you live with, who you spend time with, and what you spend your time doing are all factors in your development and its outcome.

For example, the kind of dreams and goals that some people write off as fantasies are real in my life, and they're real for the people I associate with. But they weren't real for the people I used to hang around with, the ones who sat around on the front porch, drank beer and, as my father used to say, spit at the crack in the sidewalk because they had nothing better to do.

I left those people a long time ago, and they probably didn't even realize I had gone. The change of environment was difficult at first because that had been the only life I knew. But gradually I made new friends and associates.

I have a wonderful group of friends today who help me achieve my goals. I also help them achieve theirs. We are constantly making new associations with like-minded people all over the world. That's the way it's supposed to be.

Decide what you need to adjust in your environment, and make those changes. Choose only what supports your growth. This is your responsibility, not someone else's. As Theodore Roosevelt said: "Your ability needs responsibility to expose its possibilities."

Take a piece of paper and write down on it a list of the changes you want to make in your environment. Ask yourself the following questions:

- Are you surrounded by people who support you in stepping into your highest good?

- Do you have friends who will tell you their honest perception when you cannot see a situation objectively, no matter how painful the truth may be for you to hear?

- Does your environment support you in taking time for quiet contemplation and study?

- Are the people around you constantly moving forward on their own journey to change and grow, or do they pull you back into negative perceptions of reality?

- Are you free to make changes in your life that may seem illogical to others but you know in your gut are the next steps in your personal growth?

> **You were born with access to all the Love, Security, and Self-Esteem you'll ever need.**

Answer these questions with brutal honesty. If the answer is "no" to any of them, then you must ask yourself: What in my current environment do I need to part with? How much in my environment am I willing to change in order to step into the life that my heart desires? Your willingness to let go is what ultimately determines your level of success and how completely you fulfill your potential.

Any environment that does not serve the fulfillment of your highest good is not worthy of you. But it is your job to take the steps necessary to place yourself in an environment that will lovingly support you as you step into fear and into faith.

Knowing what you know now, how could you not?

# Conclusion

Success is your birthright. Problem is, when you were growing up no one gave you the handbook on how to go about activating and choosing it. By studying the material in this book, absorbing it, and putting it into practice, you can learn to manifest what you truly want when you want it. You can create a life that reflects your highest purpose, brings joy to you, and is a blessing to others. And it doesn't need to be difficult or take a long time.

Here are some final tips, in summary:

- Trust yourself, trust Spirit, and trust in these universal laws – the main law being, More Life!

- Study to up-level your mindset and your belief system.

- No longer resist change.

- Acknowledge your pain—bring it to the light and release it, as it does not serve you.

- Accept discomfort as your best opportunity to

change, adapt, and grow.

- Have faith in yourself and in the truth that Spirit wants nothing but more life for you.

- Act boldly, let go of ego, be willing to be vulnerable, and allow Spirit to work through you.

- Embrace your divine right to receive, and know, deep in your core, that you are worthy.

- Develop the Discipline to carry it out.

It's a magnificent Universe we live in, and you're a magnificent person. You deserve abundance and magnificence in your life.

*David*

# About the Author

In September of 1989, what was supposed to be a rare relaxing day with family cruising down the Illinois River in a roomy boat, quickly turned into a nightmare...

David Neagle was pulled deep into the gates of a dam that shredded his flesh, broke his back, and nearly drowned him. No one expected him to survive the accident, and rescue workers even told his family he was already dead. (Entire boats had been sucked into this same dam, without survivors.)

What happened instead is that David, a high-school dropout & dock worker, awakened to the potential previously untapped within him. He made a decision that day to begin the journey responsible for changing his entire life, and now the lives of thousands of others.

David Neagle, Master Success & Wealth Consciousness Mentor, knows how to help you achieve whatever dream your heart desires ... no matter where you're starting from.

After his brush with death, David began to study his own potential. In the 12 months following his accident ~ despite being unable to walk for more than a month ~ he tripled his income! By December of 2000, David had expanded to become an executive corporate manager, a stock investor, and a business owner!

Over the years, David continually sought new mentors with each new level of success he attained. He began to study every great person in history ... but it wasn't until David began studying *The Science of Getting Rich*, by Wallace D. Wattles, that he fully understood the transformation he'd undergone. Wattles' book uncovered the exact change in David's thinking and in his attitude that had gotten the ball rolling; to create his unstoppable success.

*"There is nothing more important in my life ~ or in my business ~ than my own personal growth as a human being. Truly, nothing is more important to me than shedding any piece of dysfunction that would hinder me from becoming the fullest representation of Spirit's great intention for me. Nothing."* ~ David Neagle

Today, David Neagle is the President of Life is Now, Inc., a multimillion dollar global coaching practice dedicated to teaching entrepreneurs, coaches, speakers, and service providers how to use the power of Universal Law to rapidly create quantum leaps in both business and personal arenas.

Forever an avid student, David's core mission is to bring expanded awareness & higher consciousness to as many people as possible, and to find greater ways of helping entrepreneurs to create massive cash injections more rapidly, so they can lead their greatest possible lives and serve the greatest number of people.

One of the ways he's best known for doing so, is via live, in-person events. David also privately mentors his own private VIP clients to host their own transformational live events, designed to generate in excess of 7-figures in under 4 days, and simultaneously provide the opportunity for those in attendance to up-level, implement the latest proven business growth strategies & step into community with other like-minded entrepreneurs!

# A Synthesized Bibliography:

*David is an avid reader of wisdom books and synthesizes common themes among them. The endnotes listed below refer to sources for many of the specific citations used in this book.*

i   Francoise Barbira Freedman, *Water Babies*, (UK: Anness Publishing/Lorenz Books, 2001).

ii  Wallace Delois Wattles, *The Science of Getting Rich*, (USA: Elizabeth Towne, 1910).

iii Thomas Troward, *The Hidden Power* (USA: Kessinger, 2005; First published in *The Hidden Power and Other Papers on Mental Science*, USA: R.M. McBride & Co., 1921).

iv  don Miguel Ruiz, *The Voice of Knowledge*, (USA: Amber-Allen 2004).

v   Dr. John Schindler, *How to Live 365 Days a Year*, (USA: Running Press Book Publishers, 2003; First published 1956).

vi   Jesus Christ, John 8:32, *The Holy Bible: International Standard Version*® (USA: The ISV Foundation, 2008).

vii  Dr. Raymond Holliwell, *Working With the Law, Revised Ed.* (USA: DeVorss & Company, 2005; First edition, School of Christian Philosophy, 1964).

viii Genevieve Behrend, *Your Invisible Power, Revised Ed.* (USA: DeVorss & Company, 1980; First ed. USA: Elizabeth Towne, 1921).

ix   Napoleon Hill, *Think and Grow Rich,* (USA: The Ralston Society, 1937).

x    Tony Robbins, *Awaken the Giant Within,* (USA: Free Press, 1991).

xi   Napoleon Hill, *Think and Grow Rich,* (USA: The Ralston Society, 1937).

xii  Myles Munroe, *Releasing Your Potential, Expanded Edition* (USA: Destiny Image Publishers, 2007).

## Other Sources

In addition to the sources listed in the Synthesized Bibliography, David would like to acknowledge the contributions of the following other sources:

"Stickman" concept by Dr. Thurman Fleet; Dictionary definitions from www.merriam-webster.com; New Testament quotations from *The Holy Bible: International Standard Version®*, 1996-2012 by The ISV Foundation; Synopsis and dialogue from *Regarding Henry,* a Mike Nichols film, screenplay by JJ Abrams, released 1991 by Paramount Pictures (USA); Confucius quote from The Confucian Analects, as quoted on The Quotations Page, http://quotationspage.com/quote/24035.html; Plato quote as paraphrased on ThinkExist, http://thinkexist.com/quotation/life_must_be_lived_as_play/14460.html, original source Paragraph 803 from Book 7 of Plato's Laws.